AFTOSA

AFTOSA

A Historical Survey
Of Foot-and-Mouth Disease
And Inter-American Relations

Manuel A. Machado, Jr.

STATE UNIVERSITY OF NEW YORK PRESS
ALBANY

Published by State University of New York Press,
Thurlow Terrace, Albany, New York 12201

© 1969 by The Research Foundation
of State University of New York, Albany, New York

Standard Book Number 87395-040-2
Library of Congress Catalog Card Number 69-11317
Manufactured in the United States of America
Designer: Rhoda C. Curley

To My Parents,
Wife, and Children,
with affection

CONTENTS

PREFACE

A minimum level of animal protein consumption is rarely reached by most Latin Americans today; instead, vegetable protein and carbohydrates constitute the bulk of the *campesinos'* (peasants') diet. The result is protein deficiency, with its concomitant evils of malnutrition and disease. One cause of this protein lack is the prevalence of animal diseases, one of the most serious being foot-and-mouth disease (FMD or *fiebre aftosa*). Even though the disease is usually accompanied by a low mortality rate (5 to 15 per cent), in countries where it is endemic the livestock affected by the malady often number 25 to 50 per cent of the cattle population.[1] Economic losses from FMD in South America total $400 million annually, according to Pan American Foot-and-Mouth Disease Center estimates. The public health implications of this loss to the domestic market and to domestic consumption of animal protein are staggering, but despite the enormity of the problem, little is being done to effectively control the malady in the affected areas. Edgardo Seoane, former Vice-President of Peru, and Carlos Palacios, Director of the Pan American Foot-and-Mouth Disease Center in Rio de Janeiro, indicate that only two countries, Argentina and Venezuela, vaccinate as much as 80 per cent of their livestock three times a year, the minimum level for effective disease control.[2]

Informed authorities agree that only through a continental campaign can the vicious malady that threatens the entire livestock population of South America (an estimated 157,500,500 head of cattle, not counting goats, sheep, and hogs) be effectively controlled or eliminated. Such a campaign, estimates one Paraguayan authority, would cost $76,675,000 annually for an indefinite number of years in order to rid the continent of foot-and-mouth disease and to gradually expand the acceptability of South American meat on the world market.[3]

The disease is insidious, for it strikes without warning or regard for political boundaries. On any given evening, an Argentine or Venezuelan or Peruvian farmer may check his livestock and find that they are healthy. In the morning, however, some of his cattle may have soreness of the feet and mouth. As the illness progresses, the animals' temperatures may spiral upward and they may suffer excessive weight loss, decrease in milk flow, abortions, and other symptoms. Ulcerations will appear on the tongue and the soft parts of the foot, and the animal will drool copiously. The *campesino* may think, upon seeing these symptoms, that his stock has succumbed to vesicular stomatitis, or *mal de la yerba* as it is called in Mexico, a disease of much less virulence that manifests the same gross symptoms. Yet, strangely enough, the malady has failed to infect horses, mules, and burros, which are also susceptible to vesicular stomatitis, and has struck only the cloven-hoofed stock. It soon becomes apparent that the disease is *la fiebre aftosa*. The prevalence of FMD, states the Inter-American Economic and Social Council (IAECOSOC), "leads to the premature elimination of animals highly suitable for production." In addition, "the percentage is reduced of animals ready for slaughter in relation to the stock with corresponding repercussions on the meat industry and loss of employment."

Aftosa also strikes at the dairy industry, for dairy cattle are removed from production as a result of FMD infection. Even if they recover, chronic mastitis, an infection of the udder that makes the milk unfit for human consumption, often sets in and requires that some animals be slaughtered. Furthermore, cows usually abort as a result of contracting FMD and thus production for domestic markets, even at a subsistence level, is reduced.

In Latin America, an area handicapped by trade imbalances, foot-and-mouth disease makes a regularization of trade even more difficult, for countries free of the disease are loathe to trade in livestock and livestock products with nations where the disease is common.[4] Were foot-and-mouth disease merely a problem that could be dealt with on a local level, its importance to the history of inter-American relations might be negligible. Yet, its effect on trade between the United States and Latin American countries and recent efforts through the Alliance for Progress (*Alianza para el Progreso*) to bring about social and economic changes in the area necessitates a consideration of the effects of aftosa in historical perspective. The United States is no stranger to the devastation of foot-and-mouth disease. From 1870 to 1929 livestock in the United States suffered from nine outbreaks—in 1870, 1880, 1884, 1902, 1908, 1914, twice in 1924, and in 1929. Excluding the outbreak in 1929, the United States government and the governments of the affected states spent $20 million in the eradication of the disease. Moreover, 342,000 head of stock valued at $150 million were lost.[5]

Fiebre aftosa as a problem in inter-American relations must be considered in two ways: as a long-standing obstacle to the fulfillment of freer trade arrangements among the various states of the Western Hemisphere; and as a factor in the improvement of inter-American relations through the use of existing regional and international agencies and through bilateral and regional agreements. Thus far, there has been only one successful attempt to eradicate FMD in Latin America on a substantially international basis. Between 1946 and 1954 Mexico and the United States joined to defeat the virus that struck the Mexican cattle industry. Participation by the United States was motivated by national interest, for it feared that the disease would sweep northward and devastate the livestock industry of the Southwest, if not of other regions. Yet, this very complicated approach to FMD eradication brought Mexico and the United States closer together as sister republics and contributed significantly to an improvement of Mexican–United States relations.

The lesson for other countries is obvious: a realistic policy based on enlightened self-interest effectively eradicated the dread malady. The same policy could be followed by the rest of the afflicted countries of the hemisphere. Working through international and regional bodies, the nations of the hemisphere could contribute significantly to the achievement of a freer trade market in the area through the elimination of one of the greatest barriers to commercial interchange of agricultural products.

It should be noted, however, that the control of aftosa is a scientific, as well as a political, problem, for there are distinct types and subtypes of aftosa virus (Types A, O, and C). Each requires the production of a different vaccine, and bivalent or trivalent biologics have not proven as effective as the single type vaccine. Therefore, though manifesting the same gross symptoms, the virus types require different types of vaccine. For example, in a country where Type A would be prevalent, infection by Type O requires a new vaccine. By the time this is produced, the new type might be so widely spread as to cause grave difficulties in control and eradication.

For the scholar dealing with contemporary history, the difficulty of obtaining source materials is a serious handicap. Official records are often restricted for security reasons; government agencies, both in the United States and in the Latin American republics, are reluctant to release complete information without proper authority, which is difficult to obtain. Despite these problems, however, plentiful material may be obtained provided patience and persistence are exercised.

I have no complaints about either the government of the United States or those of the Latin American republics, for all have been extremely helpful in supplying materials without which this study would have been impossible. Special thanks go to Dr. Frank J. Mulhern and Dr. Donald M. Williams of the United States Department of Agriculture (USDA). Also, Dr. George L. Mehren, Assistant Secretary of Agriculture, is deserving of gratitude for his suggestions of officials to consult. The staffs of the National Agricultural Library and the National Archives were especially helpful in procuring materials for my use. The ministries of agriculture of many South Ameri-

can countries and the FMD Center in Rio de Janeiro have contributed greatly to the completion of this study through the materials
they provided. Special thanks must also go to the staff of the Benja-
min F. Feinberg Library, State University College, Plattsburgh, New
York, and to Mr. J. Richard Blanchard, Librarian, University of
California, Davis, for expeditiously supplying inter-library loan
materials.

The sections of this work dealing with Mexico were made more
valuable by the assistance of the late Dr. Fernando Camargo Núñez,
who headed the vaccine production unit of the joint United States-
Mexican effort to eradicate FMD. Dr. Donald M. Dozer, respected
advisor, colleague, and friend, read the manuscript with his usual
care and insight and offered suggestions for its improvement. The
incorporation of his criticisms have, I hope, appreciably improved the
final product. Since students are often subjected to an individual in-
structor's research, I hereby thank Mr. James T. Judge for acting as a
sounding board to my ideas on the effect of foot-and-mouth disease
on inter-American relations. Also, members of my seminars in inter-
American relations and Mexican history offered valuable commen-
tary on the manuscript. Research was carried out under the auspices
of a Grant-in-Aid in 1965–1966 and a Summer Fellowship for 1967
from the Research Foundation of State University of New York.

Preparation of the manuscript required a great deal of secretarial
and editorial patience and assistance. Therefore, I would thank my
two typists, Mrs. Becky Hollern and Miss Kaye Jacobs, for their fine
work in typing the final manuscript. To Mr. James H. Winborn, I
extend thanks for assistance in preparing an index.

Finally, I must thank my wife, Marcia M. Machado. She, too,
acted as a resonator for the writing and as a faithful bastion against
the onslaughts of our affectionate children; to them, I apologize for
being less than attentive.

Despite all of the counsel I have received, I must still assume the
responsibility for any errors of fact or interpretation that might appear.

Dallas, Texas

Manuel A. Machado, Jr.

AFTOSA

CHAPTER I

AFTOSA ENTERS LATIN AMERICA, 1870–1933

Argentina

Among the European immigrants that landed in Argentina in the late 1860's and early 1870's came an unseen passenger, the foot-and-mouth disease virus. First noted in Europe early in the sixteenth century, aftosa, in one form or another, had been a mysterious plague that debilitated European livestock. When the waves of immigrants reached Latin America in the final third of the nineteenth century, signs of foot-and-mouth disease soon became apparent in Argentina. By 1882, the disease had reached such proportions that it became an object of concern. Within twenty years the virulence of the malady attained a high degree of intensity when it appeared in Buenos Aires Province in March, 1900. Argentines, however, failed to react quickly to the menace that threatened their livestock industry. It was not until October, 1900, that the *Policía Sanitaria de los Animales* (Animal Sanitary Police) was sanctioned by law and modified later in December, 1902. Implementation of this legislation, however, was postponed until 1906 when FMD was declared an exotic disease that was to receive attention from the sanitary police.[1]

In a short time FMD began to interfere with Argentine trade. As a result of aftosa outbreaks, the Argentine government forbade the shipping of stock until the malady was at least controlled, if not eradicated. For three years (1907–1910) England embargoed Argentine stock, although an outbreak in the United Kingdom gave the Argentines an opportunity to requite and save face by closing their ports to English stock in 1910. According to the United States Legation in Buenos Aires, the Argentine citizens supported this retaliatory move.[2]

Nonetheless, livestock production remained a key industry in the Argentine economy, and despite the almost endemic presence of foot-and-mouth disease, livestock expositions continued. The cattle shows, however, proved a greater menace than benefit to the cattle industry, for the transportation of livestock to and from the fairs provided a ready means of spreading the malady from one region to another. At an international cattle exposition in Buenos Aires in 1916, it was reported that half of the stock, including some of the prizewinners, had active aftosa. This fact, however, was not revealed until after the show, and United States Consul-General William H. Robertson stated that transporting the cattle back to the different ranches would surely spread the disease.[3]

With the termination of World War I in Europe, normal trade relations among the New World Republics resumed. The United States, where FMD still struck livestock periodically, wished to join in a livestock exposition at Palermo with an exhibit of a herd of swine. United States hogs then in Montevideo, Uruguay (another FMD victim) were, of course, subject to Argentine sanitary regulations. The United States petitioned the *Sociedad Rural Argentina* (Argentine Rural Society) to inquire if it could bring pressure to bear to lighten the quarantine requirements for the swine. The Rural Society, one of the most powerful pressure groups in Argentina at the time, succeeded in having the regulations made less strict, and the hogs were shipped to Argentina for the Palermo exposition.[4]

Argentine officials had become cognizant of the international implications of foot-and-mouth disease. Thus, at the First International

Congress on Foot-and-Mouth Disease at Buenos Aires in September, 1920, it was resolved that an aftosa institute be created in that city. The actual creation of the institute, however, did not occur until 1928, and it was not inaugurated until 1939.[5]

As the virus continued to spread, Argentina again issued decrees in an attempt to control FMD. Quarantine measures were initiated, and on March 27, 1927, the government declared that no quarantine would be lifted until thirty days had elapsed without the occurrence of a single outbreak in any given region.[6]

The decrees issued by the Argentine government during the first quarter of the twentieth century were of little use and proved generally ineffective. The United States, already experienced in fighting FMD on its own soil, issued a stringent regulation (Bureau of Animal Industry, or BAI, Order 298) on September 27, 1926, that prohibited the import of chilled or frozen meat from FMD-infected countries. This order caused consternation in Argentina and aroused a good deal of hostile criticism of the United States. Argentines considered the BAI order "an unfair attempt to stifle legitimate competition" in order to benefit the United States cattle industry. To placate Argentina, the United States agreed to accept Argentine certification that meat exported to the United States came from non-infected stock. Some questions arose, however, as to the validity of the Argentine certificates, and the Department of State directed a query on the matter to the Secretary of Agriculture, who responded that Argentine certificates were acceptable to his department.[7]

The United States' concession to the contrary notwithstanding, Argentine tempers remained aroused by BAI Order 298. One Argentine veterinarian declared that the embargo did not, in fact, apply to Argentina because that nation had already complied with the requirements of the order by demanding that owners provide certification that cattle came from areas free of FMD for at least thirty days prior to slaughter. In addition, he noted that slaughter occurred without contact with infected stock. The BAI order also aggravated the Argentine trade balance with the United States, which was already unfavorable, and "nourished a growing antipathy" toward the United States. Argentina bought two-and-one-half times more from the United States than the United States purchased in Argentina. After the BAI order, bilateral trade was further impaired because of the prohibition on livestock and meat shipments. When the British Parliamentary Secretary of Agriculture and Fisheries arrived in Buenos Aires in 1928, it was noted that tact and diplomacy on the part of the Englishman smoothed the way for his suggestions on the improvement of the Argentine livestock problem. United States Ambassador Robert Woods Bliss stated that "the contrast between these conditions [engendered by the British official] and the unfriendly sentiments aroused in Argentina last year by the brusque methods used by the United States Department of Agriculture cannot fail but to give occasion for serious reflection." [8]

Anti-Americanism persisted in Argentina when the USDA added Argentine exports of grapes and alfalfa to its list of prohibited items coming from FMD areas because these could act as carriers for FMD virus. Ambassador Bliss stated that if Argentina could feel reasonably certain of a market for 100,000 tons of chilled beef in the United States, the Argentines' anger would be reduced. "She would," he wrote, "look to the United States as a friend rather than a nation whose government is inclined to place obstacles in Argentina's way of selling her surplus produce. . . ." [9]

By October, 1928, Hipólito Irigoyen, the "Father of the People," came to power a second time. He entered the presidency in an atmosphere of hostility toward the United States that, though ameliorated, could flare up again. Ambassador Bliss advised that though the furor caused by the BAI order was quiescent,

> it could be easily aroused, and . . . our government should prevent, at the beginning of the present Argentine administration, an action on our part that would tend to cause the new Government to be influenced by wide spread anti-American sentiment. Our enemies in this country are plentiful, and though they are much less active . . . they would gladly seize an opportunity to arouse dormant susceptibilities.[10]

Argentina, however, recognized that a good deal of the livestock problem she faced needed domestic and regional solution. Still dependent on British markets, Argentina, Brazil, and Uruguay entered into an agreement with Great Britain to reduce the risk of "transferring foot-and-mouth disease in carcass meat and offal from South America." The agreement covered the certification of *frigoríficos* (packinghouses), the inspection of animals and vehicles en route to market, and the inspection of livestock on the hoof. It was also agreed that no animal from a herd containing active infection would be slaughtered for export and all packings and wrappings would be new.[11]

The gravity of foot-and-mouth disease was discussed at the Sixth Inter-American Conference of American States held at Havana, Cuba, between January 16 and February 28, 1928. Argentina, in the forefront of opposition to assertedly arbitrary sanitary measures, proposed to the conference that it

> take measures to reduce high customs barriers which hamper the freedom of circulation of commerce of agricultural products [and that such barriers] be eliminated with respect to those articles in which such elimination does not constitute a danger to the vital interests of the country and its workers; *and that for the purpose of exercising the rights of sanitary police and plant quarantine the signatory countries adopt an organic rule guaranteeing that the measures that might be taken should in no case be of an arbitrary nature.*

The resolution failed to garner enough votes for passage. The Conference, however, did resolve that another inter-American conference be held in January, 1929, to deal specifically with plant and animal sanitary control. The proposed meeting would be charged with the establishment of uniformity in methods for combating and preventing plant and animal diseases in the member states through either individual or collective action. In addition, the countries were to develop criteria regarding quarantine, fumigation, disinfections and exclusion of stock dependent upon the possibility of transmission, contamination, and the rate at which the various plagues acclimated. Furthermore, the problem of admitting stock imports that might be contaminated, susceptible to plagues, or vehicles for parasitary diseases was to be discussed. Moreover, the new conference was charged with the study of the creation of an Inter-American Board of Agricultural Defense.[12]

During the time of the Havana Conference, Britain brought pressure to bear on Argentina for increased British-Argentine trade. Argentina, however, indicated a decided preference for trade with the United States, despite the United States embargo on Argentine meats. Yet, the officials of the Platine Republic felt that unless the United

States revised some of its more prohibitive tariff policies, they would be forced to cut trade and turn commercial attentions to the United Kingdom.[13]

More decrees emanated from Argentina in an attempt to reduce the occurrence of FMD. On May 2, 1928, the Minister of Agriculture ordered that all FMD outbreaks must be reported and prohibited the transit of sick animals. By February 9 of the following year, the Ministerial decree was modified to allow the application of fines for violation of the regulation.[14]

Meanwhile, the United States was to suffer from one more outbreak of aftosa. In November, 1928, the *City of Los Angeles* docked at Buenos Aires for provisions, including chilled Argentine meat. But when it arrived in California it was unable to unload the meat at San Pedro. The ship officials, therefore, ordered the meat trimmed for shipment elsewhere, and the scraps went into garbage, which was sold raw as hog swill. Shortly thereafter hog farmers in the Los Angeles area reported outbreaks of a highly virulent vesicular disease that proved to be FMD. The source was finally discovered when a broken piece of crockery bearing the legend *City of Los Angeles* was located at one of the infected farms.[15]

During the spring of 1929, it was generally believed that all un-cooked meat could carry FMD, and the BAI proposed the restriction of fowl imports from FMD countries. The Department of State noted that it had no objections to the proposed restriction but hoped that "it can be promulgated in such a way as to forestall the attempts which will probably be made to show that instead of a sanitary regulation it is really a disguised form of protection for the American poultry industry." Noting the latent anti-Americanism extant in Argentina, the Department of State declared that "this order will give the anti-American propagandists a fine opportunity to raise the old cry which caused so much trouble a couple of years ago. . . ."[16]

In 1929, the world-wide depression began to disturb the already precarious trade balance between the United States and the rest of the world. The United States was forced to retrench and to establish tariff barriers for the protection of its suffering industries. BAI Order 298 served as an effective barrier against unwanted competition from Argentina and other meat-producing countries. Before 1926 Argentina had not been a great exporter of meat to the United States, even though the Underwood Tariff Act of 1913 removed duties on meats. Some trade developed during this time, only to be interrupted by World War I. By 1922, the Fordney-McCumber Tariff Act restored duties on meats. The *coup de grâce* to Argentine hopes for meat trade with the United States came with Section 306 (a) of the Smoot-Hawley Tariff Act of 1930. Prior to the passage of the tariff act of 1930, Congressional discussion indicated that little was known about FMD by the public. Rumors abounded that the meat might not be fit for human consumption and that the malady was transferrable to human beings. Upon the announcement of the Smoot-Hawley tariff to the various embassies in Washington, the Argentine Rural Society held an "indignation meeting" to ascertain what could be done to counter the United States action. The Rural Society strongly supported a policy of "buy from those who buy from us" and pledged themselves to withdraw large tracts of land from cattle production and to plant cereals with which to compete with the United States more effectively. The threat, however, was not carried out.[17]

While BAI Order 298 gave the Secretary of Agriculture some discretionary powers, the Smoot-Hawley tariff specifically mandated that he bar certain meat and animal products from any FMD-infected country. Already the so-called embargo of 1926 had effectively discontinued meat and meat product imports from Argentina, Brazil, Paraguay, Uruguay, and some European countries. Argentina, proud of its meat inspection system and its beef industry, declared that the embargo and the tariff act of 1930 were not merely a matter of the economic blow to its industry. Argentines' pride was injured by what they thought to be an obvious policy on the part of the United States to protect its own domestic industry. One United States senator, during the debate that whirled around the Smoot-Hawley tariff, clearly indicated his interpretation of the discriminatory nature of Section 306 (a).[18]

Argentina realized the futility of trying to combat the law of 1930 and attempted a different tack. The Argentine ambassador to the United States argued that the term "country" in Section 306 (a) should be interpreted in a geographical rather than a political sense. He contended that Tierra del Fuego was, in fact, a geographic country separate from the Argentine Republic. Moreover, sheep, the principal livestock of that area, were less susceptible to FMD than other cloven-hoofed animals. "Thanks to this fact," he wrote, "and the geographic isolation of the region—Patagonia—from the other cattle regions of the country, the sheep flocks of the territories of Santa Cruz and Tierra del Fuego are absolutely free from rinderpest and foot-and-mouth disease. . . ." [19]

The legal advisor of the Department of State was soon presented with the vexatious position initiated by the Argentine ambassador. The issue hinged on whether or not the United States could import frozen meat from Patagonia on the basis of the most-favored nation clause of the treaty of 1853 with Argentina despite Article VIII of the Sanitary Convention of 1928 with Mexico (see Appendix) and Section 306 (a) of the 1930 tariff. The legal department decided that Article VIII of the treaty with Mexico did not apply because it mentioned only livestock and animal by-products, not frozen meat. It was noted, however, that if Article VIII of the treaty were made applicable, written assurances from the Argentine government that it would observe all obligations required of Mexico under the treaty were necessary. It was doubted that Argentina would accept those conditions. [20]

At the Pan American Commercial Conference of October, 1931, Argentina—supported by Brazil, Chile, and Uruguay—applied to the United States for a reduction of tariff barriers. The supporters of the appeal implied that desire for sanitary precautions was not so determining as was an insistence for economic protectionism in the decision to adopt Section 306 (a) of the tariff of 1930. [21] The Argentine delegation suggested that the United States feared competition from the Platine Republic because the production costs on the Río de la Plata were lower and would drive down the price of meat in the United States. Argentina also advanced its geographic argument, citing the United Kingdom (England, Northern Ireland, Scotland, and Wales) as a perfect example of distinct geographic entities joined politically. In a resolution that was ultimately accepted, the Conference recommended that sanitary regulations must not be of a protective nature and that "infected zones" be used instead of "infected countries" in determining the acceptability of animal and animal by-product importations. [22]

Direct appeals from Argentine Ambassador Felipe Espil that some areas of Argentina be declared free of infection became another part of Argentine strategy. Espil based his argument on the zone thesis found in the treaty of 1928 with Mexico. Unfortunately, the Secretary of Agriculture informed the Department of State that the zone theory was, in fact, a fiction. The central problem revolved around whether or not meat from central Argentina went south for domestic consumption or whether Patagonia was a self-sufficient entity. If the south were not dependent on central Argentina, it might be possible to import some Patagonian mutton. Espil's efforts won him support in Buenos Aires, and editorial comment in *La Prensa,* and *La Nación* strongly criticized what they argued was United States protectionism. *La Prensa* of November 15, 1931, declared:

> Our ambassador in that country would do well to maintain his vigilant attitude of energetic protection in the face of the lack of veracity which constitutes the basis of the measures adopted by the Government of the United States and to affirm his attitude further he should document himself with the precedents we have mentioned. . . . A categorical declaration must be made once and for all in order to prevent the repetition of these truly censurable doings to the discredit of Argentine products.[23]

Argentine hopes for a relaxation of the quarantine restrictions continued into 1932. Nonetheless, Dr. S. O. Fladness of the BAI frankly stated that Section 306 (a) was clearly protectionist and that United States cattlemen were motivated as much by their desire to impose a prohibitive tariff as by their fear of FMD. He acknowledged they would bring tremendous pressures to bear on the USDA if it attempted to reinterpret the wording of the tariff of 1930.[24]

As depression continued to engulf the Western Hemisphere, Argentina found itself forced to negotiate what Argentine public opinion considered a humiliating agreement with the United Kingdom. The Roca-Runciman Pact of May 1, 1933, placed Argentina in a position of exempting foreign exchange obtained from exports to Great Britain except for "a reasonable sum" to be set aside for the service of the Argentine foreign debt. In return, Great Britain gave a qualified guarantee that it would not reduce its imports of Argentine chilled beef below the levels of 1932 unless it was necessary for the good of the United Kingdom. The Roca-Runciman Pact proved to be a triumph of the "buy from those who buy from us" policy so strongly advocated by the Argentine Rural Society. It failed, however, to satisfy many of the beef barons who still hoped to break into the United States market.[25] Argentina, therefore, was forced into a position whereby she could salvage at least a part of her beef commerce, and Argentine cattlemen would have to wait for another try at the coveted United States market.

Mexico

During the long period of time when Argentina was groping for a solution to FMD and for a wedge into the United States market, Mexico and the United States became involved in a series of quiet maneuvers that would eventually lead to the signing of a sanitary convention between the two countries in 1928. In 1913 in Tampico the United States Consul there warned that the area was possibly enzoötic with aftosa. The information was transmitted to the USDA, which in turn asked the Department of State to arrange for a government veterinarian to visit the Tampico area to ascertain the validity of the consul's assertion. The veterinarian ultimately determined that aftosa was not the problem; he did, however, note that Tampico suffered from an abysmal lack of veterinary or sanitary control facilities. The United States, of course, was concerned, for many cattle from FMD countries entered Mexico and were moved to northern Mexico, placing the United States cattle industry in jeopardy. Up to this time, Mexico had remained free of FMD, and the United States hoped to maintain Mexico as a buffer between itself and the areas where the malady was endemic.[26]

The initial aftosa scare in Mexico of 1913 was merely the beginning of over a decade of concern in the United States with this potential problem in Mexico. Another instance in 1915 brought Texans and Mexicans to loggerheads when Texas imposed an embargo on any cattle brought in from Mexico. In 1922, a report from Nuevo Laredo reached the Department of State that Argentine cattle were entering Mexico through the Gulf ports. Inquiries made of all consulates indicated that the report was false. The consuls at both Nuevo Laredo and at Veracruz agreed, however, that much of the report might have been based on propaganda effectively planted by Southwestern cattlemen in an attempt to keep Argentina from capitalizing on Mexico's need for livestock. The first decade of the Mexican

Revolution had thoroughly decimated Mexico's livestock herds, and she needed new breeding stock that was more reasonably priced than that found in the United States.[27]

United States cattlemen strongly supported the idea of an agreement between Mexico and the United States to prevent the introduction into either country of animals and animal products originating in FMD areas. The USDA supported the proposal, and the subsequent events underscored the necessity of a sanitary convention between Mexico and the United States. Two outbreaks of aftosa occurred in the United States in 1924. In February an outbreak of supposed Oriental origin struck California livestock and gave support to the imperative nature of an agreement between the two neighboring countries. In September, Texas livestock suffered an outbreak of aftosa that caused Mexico to quarantine all Texas stock coming from the afflicted counties.[28]

Within eighteen months (1926) of the Texas outbreak, Mexico shared in the FMD problem, for Tabasco livestock became infected with a virus of unknown origin. The United States suspended importation of all livestock and livestock products from the infected area. Moreover, some United States authorities and interested private citizens feared that eradication measures in Tabasco might not be vigorously pursued in view of the growing power and potential opposition of the Garrido Canabal family, which controlled the political machinery of the area. Yet despite the problems faced by Mexico in the eradication of the malady, within a year after the outbreak, the country was declared free of FMD.[29]

The outbreaks occurring in the United States in 1924 and in Mexico in 1926 firmly pointed to the need for a sanitary convention. Even during the intensely nationalistic early phase of the administration of President Plutarco Elías Calles, Mexican enthusiasm for such a convention was apparent. Within a year, however, the enthusiasm had dissipated because, as one observer asserted, Mexico had yielded to pressures from other Latin American governments which hoped to find a market for their livestock in Mexico. Mexico still needed livestock to replenish her depleted herds, and she began to look to South America for a possible source of supply. In 1926, the Argentine Rural Society arranged for an exposition of Argentine livestock in Mexico City. Reportedly, special care was exercised in the transport and handling of the stock, and after Mexican breeders had seen those animals the latter were promptly returned to Argentina. The United States, however, was not deterred in its efforts. One official advised that before Mexico entered into any negotiations with the United States it must be evident to the world that it did so of its own volition and not as a result of pressures from the north.[30]

During the Tabasco outbreak the impasse finally broke. Mexican and United States negotiators, with the support of United States cattlemen, met in Washington in July, 1926. In the following month, a set of resolutions were prepared for approval by both governments. By March 16, 1928, the final treaty was signed. The United States Senate ratified the treaty on March 28, but over a year passed before Mexico gave its assent. On January 17, 1930, both governments exchanged ratifications, and the treaty went into effect the next day.[31]

The key articles, VIII and IX, of the treaty that caused Argentina to attempt to enter the United States market read as follows (see Appendix for entire text of treaty):

ARTICLE VIII

The livestock sanitary officials shall define the specific territory in their respective countries in which any contagious or infectious disease exists and shall indicate zones which may be considered as exposed, in order to prevent the propagation and dissemination of the infection of such disease.

ARTICLE IX

The High Contracting Particles shall not issue permits for domestic ruminants or swine originating in any foreign countries or zones where highly infectious and rapidly spreading diseases such as foot-and-mouth disease and rinderpest appear frequently, until at least sixty days have elapsed without any outbreak of the disease in such countries or zones. When a disease of this kind occurs in any part of a foreign country any other part of the same country shall be considered as exposed until the contrary is positively shown, that is, until it is shown that no communication exists between the two parts by which the disease may be readily transmitted. When such a disease occurs near the land border of a foreign country the neighboring part of the adjacent country shall be considered as exposed until the contrary is positively shown.[32]

Thus, Mexico and the United States took a decisive step in preventing foot-and-mouth disease from entering their territories. The treaty, however, was a marriage of convenience, for both countries violated the convention and ultimately a disastrous outbreak of FMD would occur in Mexico in December, 1946 (See Chapters III and IV).

Peru and Chile

While the majestic, snowcapped Andean cordillera might seem a perfect natural barrier against *la fiebre aftosa,* such was not the case. By 1910 unconfirmed reports reached the U.S. State Department that FMD had entered Peru. Again in late 1923 the Secretary of Agriculture communicated with the Secretary of State and informed him of the possible existence of FMD in Peru. Even though no official reports confirmed the presence of the malady, the USDA requested that the consulates inquire as to its alleged appearance. The Consulate General in Peru reported in February 1924 that the vesicular disease in question was FMD. He reported that it seemed to be benign, although nearly three thousand cases had been reported. It was suggested that the Peruvian Minister of Fomento (Development) receive all pertinent data that the USDA had available on FMD.[33]

Meanwhile, as early as 1914, the cattle industry of Chile had begun to decline. Cattle importations from Argentina allowed the Chileans to put their land to other uses and made Chile more dependent on cattle imports for meat supplies. Chile, however, was already aware of the FMD problem because in 1910 she published a *Cartilla* (brochure) for the edification of Chilean farmers. The publication described aftosa and the measures required to avoid it.[34]

Chilean importation of potentially exposed and infected stock from Argentina eventually had adverse effects, despite the organization of an Animal Sanitary Police in December, 1924. Mild and severe outbreaks occurred throughout the 1920's, and in 1930 a wave of aftosa of large proportions swept the north-central regions of Chile. As early as January 25, 1930, the United States Consul at Antofagasta reported that at least one focus of FMD existed within 144 kilometers of his Consular district. It was believed that the disease had been introduced by livestock imports from Argentina. USDA officials quickly recognized that Chile should be listed among the afflicted countries, and when the Chilean steamship *Aconcagua* landed in New

York City, it was noted that it carried meat scraps from meat obtained in Chile. The captain was informed by USDA officials that the scraps must be dumped at sea or incinerated aboard ship. Under no circumstance could scraps be landed on United States soil.[35]

Uruguay

Back in the Río de la Plata, FMD also appeared in Uruguay. In June, 1910, the Department of Soriano reported infection, and the *Diario Oficial* acknowledged the presence of the malady. Exportation of stock from Soriano Province was prohibited. Only stock from Montevideo, Paipándu, and Colônia were allowed exportation. Within two weeks after the report of FMD in Soriano, the Department of Rivera also noted the presence of disease, and the Minister of the Interior reported the fact to the United States Consul at Montevideo. Within a month, however, President Guillermo Wílliman declared Soriano free of FMD. With the declaration, fat stock began moving toward Montevideo for shipment.[36]

Conditions in Uruguay, however, failed to improve. BAI Inspector S. O. Fladness reported that meat leaving Rio Grande do Sul, Brazil, for market in Montevideo, was sent to inferior packinghouses with unsanitary conditions. Fladness noted that certification authenticated by the United States Consul at Rio Grande do Sul was necessary before the meat could be transshipped to the United States.[37]

During the passage of a decade, conditions continued to deteriorate. FMD spread throughout the República Oriental del Uruguay. In preparation for the visit of the British Minister of Agriculture, investigations were initiated regarding Uruguayan sanitary precautions. At first they seemed adequate, but under closer scrutiny were found "worthless and superficial." Doubts were raised that FMD could be eradicated in Uruguay even within ten years.[38]

Brazil

Just north of Uruguay stands South America's giant, Brazil, a country that also failed to escape the scourge of FMD. The disease was first reported in 1895 in Uberaba. Before that time infection was unknown in either Minas Gerais or São Paulo. It was also noted that for some reason the malady seemed to be less virulent than its European counterparts. Within a short number of years, the virus spread generally throughout Brazil, concentrating, however, in São Paulo and Minas Gerais. The campaign against FMD in Brazil in 1910 centered primarily on the southern sections of the country, and some exports to Argentina and Uruguay continued. FMD apparently struck fear in local cattle raisers and in the populace of Pará in general. Pará's main beef source was Argentina, but because of FMD the people ceased buying Argentine meat and were supported in the boycott by local producers. In São Paulo, an education campaign began in 1913 to inform the people of the measures to combat FMD and to acquaint them with the nature of the disease. The publication of a pamphlet entitled *A Febre Aphtosa* was the principal means of disseminating information.[39]

FMD moved north to Pernambuco by 1916, and as a result of an outbreak, no hides were shipped to the United States. In 1919, the United States Consul there reported that he allowed hides to go to the United States, but they had been collected before the outbreak. He noted that shippers were required to bear the expense of disinfection if so required by the USDA. The USDA, in turn, informed the Secretary of State that shipment of green or dried hides was permissable provided that no infection existed in the area of origin and also recommended that the consul at Pernambuco check BAI regulations regarding hide shipments.[40]

Hide shipments and FMD also caused problems in Rio Grande do Sul in 1919. The state had widespread infection, and the United States Consul at Porto Alegre recommended that only dried hides, not green ones, be shipped to the United States. In addition, all hides taken after July 15 required disinfection. The gravity of the disease was readily apparent when it became common at slaughter houses. Veterinary inspection was a "farce" because most inspectors were not veterinarians; rather, they were practicing medical doctors with political influence who received the inspection posts as sinecures while they continued to practice medicine. The result was that all hides, regardless of place of origin, required disinfection because of the highly inadequate inspection procedures.[41]

Brazilians, as proud of their livestock industry as were the Argentines, hoped to exhibit Zebu stock at an exposition in the United States and sought permission in 1922 from the Secretary of Agriculture to bring animals into the United States. The USDA, however, denied Brazil permission to bring in its Zebus because it wanted to protect the United States against aftosa.[42] Brazil, like Argentina, continued in its attempts to obtain a lifting of the United States quarantine. The Brazilian Ambassador, upon instructions from his government, requested that restrictions on livestock and livestock products from São Paulo be lifted. He claimed that the malady was eradicated. The USDA, however, responded that it could not give "favorable consideration" to the Brazilian request.[43]

Soon it became apparent that Brazil hoped to sell Zebu stock in Mexico. In the spring of 1923 it was learned that a shipment was on its way to Mexico via New Orleans, and the USDA Inspector in charge at New Orleans was instructed to prohibit debarkation of the animals that might carry aftosa. It was noted, however, that nothing could prevent the animals from landing at Veracruz, Mexico. The only way such a situation could be avoided would be for the bulls to debark at New Orleans. At this point, the Inspector could legitimately require a quarantine period and a series of laboratory diagnoses.[44]

Aftosa continued to take its toll in Brazil. Minas Gerais reported more outbreaks in 1923. The Brazilians again requested that Brazilian cattle be allowed to enter the United States and were again given a negative response. However, Brazilian bulls would land at Veracruz in 1924, and the threat to the United States cattle industry was more serious because the three hundred Zebus apparently were eventually destined for Galveston, Texas. Mexico would become a way-station for Brazilian sales of Zebus to Texas breeders.[45]

Foot-and-mouth disease in Brazil in the 1920's engendered a few "quack" ideas to eradicate the malady. The most notable incident came from one Count Fernando de Lusino, who claimed to have a cure for FMD in which the USDA might be interested. The USDA, however, responded negatively, asserting that experimentation was not allowed in the United States because of the virulence of the disease. Moreover, the USDA affirmed its faith in the slaughter method for eradication of the malady. The United States Consul at Porto Alegre informed the Count that the USDA was not interested and further noted:

. . . in a conversation two days ago with the Assistant Mayor of this city, Senhor Alberto Bins, who is the owner of a large stock ranch, . . . I was informed by him that Count Fernando de Lusino had not demonstrated satisfactorily to him the efficacy of his remedy. It seems that the Count lays particular stress on the bridle and bit that he uses . . . for administering the liquid. . . .

The attempts of the Count and two associates for the organization of a company in Brazil to manufacture the elixir, bridle, and bit failed to materialize. The Consul further added:

> . . . due to lack of evidence of the efficacy of the remedy, to some of the questionable associates of the Count, and his extreme eagerness to ally a man of Senhor Bins' social and financial standing with his company, there has been considerable distrust created regarding the Count and his remedy for foot-and-mouth disease.[46]

During the period between 1870 and 1933, FMD was a menace throughout the greater part of Latin America and in the United States. It swept into Uruguay, Brazil, Chile, Peru, the United States, and Mexico. The reasons for its spread are apparent: lack of general knowledge about the nature of the disease on the part of government officials; stockraisers who were ignorant of the disease and its remedy; and governmental ineptitude. These circumstances contributed to what appeared to some as an ambivalent position of the United States about FMD in Latin America. Only in the 1920's did the United States seem to become firm in its desire to keep the disease outside of its territorial limits and out of its nearest neighboring country, Mexico. Actually, the United States officials had two complementary objectives. On the one hand, the USDA upheld the highest known standards of regulation and control. On the other hand, they were supported by United States cattle raisers' intent, in part, to keep competition from South America out of the United States market. The sanitary convention with Mexico was a positive step taken toward cooperative prevention and control of foot-and-mouth disease. That maneuver, however, would prove a Pyrrhic victory.

CHAPTER II

THE GOOD NEIGHBOR AND WAR, 1933–1946

Argentina

With the hemisphere engulfed in a disastrous depression that dislocated the economies of the New World and produced more political instability in Latin America, marked changes occurred in United States attitudes toward its southern neighbors. The Administration of Franklin D. Roosevelt proposed a so-called "Good Neighbor Policy" specifically designed to keep the United States out of Latin American affairs and to contribute to hemispheric harmony. It soon became apparent that Roosevelt would willingly make concessions, especially to the Argentine giant, to uphold his Good Neighbor Policy. In addition, Argentina was more involved than any other republic in the conflict between desires of livestock raisers in the United States to keep South American meat out of the country and South American wishes to break into the United States markets.

Very early in the Roosevelt Administration, the President and his advisors accepted the Argentine view of Section 306 (a) of the Smoot-Hawley tariff by giving it an interpretation based on the zone theory. Argentina, moreover, found "awakening hope" in the return of the Democratic Party to power, especially when faced with the probability of a curtailment of British imports of Argentine beef.[1] Embassy officials, Argentine newspapers reported, implied that United States officials had intimated to the Argentine legation in Washington that they might allow entry of chilled and frozen beef in return for tariff concessions, a maneuver outside the limits imposed by the Smoot-Hawley tariff. This intimation, however, gave unwarranted optimism to the Argentines, for Ambassador Espil understood it to mean that the United States had promised a satisfactory solution to the meat problem. Espil wrote to Cordell Hull, Secretary of State, expressing confidence that "when the matter is examined with high and serene impartiality by the new authorities of your Department and the Department of Agriculture, they will find it easy to give satisfaction to my Government's legitimate request." Such, however, was not the case, for the only promise made to Espil was that the United States would send experts to Argentina to study the problem.[2]

Hull and his Department began attempts to get a clear revision of the 1930 law in accordance with Administration policy of "removing restrictions of trade" and improving relations by the elimination of friction. The Attorney General's office, however, ruled against the State Department for attempting to usurp legislative functions. According to one scholar, the State Department was "frustrated by this legal opinion on geography and legislative intent."[3]

Negotiations and attempts to explain the United States' position were underway in early 1934. Spruille Braden, then on one of many diplomatic missions for the Department of State, informed Hull that in a conversation with Leopoldo Melo, Argentine Minister of the Interior and Agriculture, he had informed the minister of Hull's intent to reexamine sanitary restrictions. At the same time, Melo was told of interest group pressures in the United States.[4] Argentina, however, still hoped for a bilateral trade agreement with the United States, but by the end of the year a new and more extensive wave of FMD struck Argentine livestock. The new infection apparently started in the spring of 1934 in northern Argentina and in Uruguay and spread throughout Buenos Aires Province. The Ministry of Agriculture initiated measures to keep the infection under control and, in an attempt to isolate the disease, closed down affected establishments. By December, 1934, the quarantine measures had taken their toll on the market, for meat prices began to rise because of a reduced number of cattle arriving at the slaughterhouse.[5]

Argentina, despite the intensification of its aftosa problem, looked favorably upon the disposition of the new Administration in Washington to work out an agreement for Argentine meat from disease-free zones. *La Nación* of Buenos Aires recognized the pressures imposed on the United States by farm and livestock groups but still nourished the hope of a trade agreement and a modification of tariff restrictions. At the same time, the State Department initiated quiet negotiations with Argentina for a sanitary convention. Hull's subordinates, however, felt it impossible to determine the reception such a treaty would receive in the Senate and noted that cattle interests "may oppose it as a 'back door' attempt to amend Section 306. . . ." Exporters and manufacturers, however, probably would lend support if informed of the treaty, for they stood to gain in terms of increased exports to Argentina. Their pressure might counter that of the livestock interests, and, it was hoped, the treaty would possibly slip through the Senate in 1935. Precedents already existed for the proposed sanitary convention with Argentina. A trade treaty with Brazil signed in 1935 and the sanitary convention with Mexico gave hope to Argentine and State Department officials for the successful consummation of a mutually satisfactory treaty. It was noted, however, that the treaty with Mexico was not "a precise precedent," for it sought to prevent the introduction into Mexico of stock from FMD countries, not to restrict the importation of Mexican stock into the United States. The Mexican convention did establish the principle in Article VIII "that there may be a third country in which foot-and-mouth exists, zones which are free from contagion and from which cattle and by-products thereof may be imported." [6]

The sanitary convention signed with Argentina on May 24, 1935, proved to be an attempt on the part of Hull and FDR to improve trade and political relations with the Platine Republic. Both Roosevelt and Hull argued that under Article III of the recently signed treaty North American interests were amply protected, for it provided that each country possessed a fundamental right to restrict importations from areas considered infected. Moreover, the treaty fulfilled the resolution adopted at the Fourth Pan American Commercial Conference of October, 1931, for it provided that santiary police regulations would not have the character of protective customs measures. Hull added that "the approval of this convention will do much toward strengthening friendly intercourse between the United States and Argentina, . . . without impairing the sovereign right of either government to impose sanitary measures deemed necessary . . . for the protection of its livestock and agricultural interests." Roosevelt further indicated that Article III (see Appendix for text of treaty) operated to prevent the "use of sanitary regulations as a disguised means of restriction of importation for protective purposes. . . ." [7]

Immediate reaction in Argentina to the convention proved favorable. "They are apparently particularly gratified," wrote the United States Ambassador, "at the removal, if only in part, of what they have looked upon as a stigma against Argentina the effect of which . . . has been a source of irritation." Not only would the convention improve relations between the two countries, but it would also serve as a means of "releasing Argentina from her dependence upon Great Britain—the chief market for its meat exports." Dr. Carlos Saavedra Lamas, Argentine Foreign Minister, rhapsodized that the pact signified "an old desire of our livestock industry to which it brings a legitimate moral satisfaction." *Noticias Gráficas* of Buenos Aires pointed out that only Senatorial ratification remained and added:

> We believe that they cannot refuse to do so, no matter what pressure may be brought to bear upon same by cattle-raising interests. To refuse to ratify this treaty would be to recognize that the importation of Argentine meat is prohibited owing to the demands of a commercial war, which are at variance with the good relations that we maintain with the great Republic of the North.[8]

When news of the sanitary convention reached United States livestock interests, various stock raisers' associations inundated the State Department with protests. The treaty was viewed as ill-conceived, and it was hoped that it would be quickly put down by the Senate.[9] Yet, despite initial opposition, the State Department found powerful allies in the National Foreign Trade Council and the Argentine-American Chamber of Commerce, which sent a brief to the Senate

Foreign Relations Committee stating that the convention would not harm United States interests. One leading entrepreneur wrote that "American exporters, and exporters as a whole, approve the action which has been taken, and, as always, we are desirous of giving you any support or assistance you may desire." He also noted that "the embargo on Argentine meats was the basis of much of the anti-American propaganda in that country. . . ."[10]

The Bureau of Animal Industry, hesitant to participate in policy decisions, nevertheless refused to support the treaty. During the negotiations of the convention, Dr. John R. Mohler, BAI Chief, and his staff gave technical advice, but when supporters were sought for ratification, Mohler and his staff remained aloof, despite the pleadings of Hull and the State Department.[11]

Failure of the Senate to give rapid ratification to the convention provoked critical comment in Argentina throughout the summer of 1935. Buenos Aires newspapers noted the existence of pressures on the Senate aimed at the defeat of the convention. *El Diario* of Buenos Aires commented that the sanitary convention was

> evident proof that the United States desired to create the impression that it is disposed to do us justice by raising the embargo on our livestock but this was merely an impression. Actually, we will obtain nothing as congressional opposition will not be overcome by the good intentions of President Roosevelt.

In a retaliatory vein *La Prensa* of that same city noted, somewhat sarcastically,

> United States distrust leads us to suspect that as a justification we should create an analogous defense. Germs are spread by various means, both animate and inanimate. It could be easily explained that as a sanitary precaution Argentina might find inconvenient the introduction of machinery and motors, in general, manufactured articles, as carrying germs not only dangerous to livestock but to the inhabitants of the country.[12]

Throughout the summer opposition to the treaty in sections of the United States mounted. Representatives and senators from Western, beef-producing states registered their protests with the Department of State, and state legislatures in the West passed a series of resolutions roundly condemning the treaty and the State Department. Patagonia, the disease-free area, appeared to one congressman as "an entering wedge." This same congressman stressed "the economic angle," declaring that,

> This is a quarantine device used as an economic barrier. Everyone in this country has known it for years, but it seems to me a good device, and that it has served a good purpose and still is serving a good purpose.

Moreover, after the announcement of the treaty, cattle prices fell in various United States stockyards.[13]

Opposition to the convention peaked by the end of summer 1935. Hull, however, "determined to enter upon a vigorous campaign of education." The treaty was given wide circulation, and thousands of copies of it and an accompanying letter went out stating that the importation of Patagonian mutton would be negligible. Moreover, Hull emphasized the discriminatory nature of Section 306 (a). Reports reaching the State Department from Buenos Aires indicated that it was not "anticipated that a sudden taste will develop in the American consuming market for mutton. The seasons for processing in Patagonia cannot be made to coincide with the most attractive mid-winter purchasing period in the United States." This report gave Hull justification for his statement.[14]

Hull's education campaign failed to reduce Congressional and livestock raisers' opposition to the treaty. Cattle interests argued that the embargo was not, in fact, discriminatory.[15] The *American Cattle Producer,* official organ of the American National Livestock Association, asserted the argument that Argentine meat imports were made necessary by a shortage in the United States was fallacious. Moreover, warned that journal, free trade advocates in the USDA and the State Department would allow importation from Patagonia, which in turn would open floodgates of infection to the United States.[16]

Despite the failure of ratification in 1935, when Franklin Roosevelt sailed to Buenos Aires for the Inter-American Conference in November, 1936, he was acclaimed by the Argentines. Moreover, he left them with the heady wine of United States renunciation of intervention, a promise of consultative procedures, and an implied promise of ratification of the sanitary convention. The United States Ambassador reported:

> The President leaves behind him a people whose sentiments and whose imagination he has captured. If the affections he has won are strengthened by the ratification of the Sanitary Convention, and by eagerly hoped for American concessions to Argentine trade, there is no doubt but that the relations between the United States and the southern republic will experience a great and lasting improvement. On the other hand, should the hopes now aroused be disappointed it is to be anticipated that the effects of the visit will be seriously weakened.

Unanimity for the extraordinary conference did not exist. Felipe Espil fervently hoped to postpone the meeting until the convention was ratified and threatened that without ratification the "entire Argentine attitude on Pan-Americanism would change." Another Argentine further argued that United States restrictions continued to stigmatize Argentine meat products and produce bad publicity for Argentina on the world market. Ratification of the treaty would remove the stigma and would prove to the Argentine people that the United States was not delivering false promises.[17]

Treaty supporters in the State Department continued their campaign to win over livestock interests in favor of the controversial convention. They argued that embargoes on stock from uninfected areas in otherwise infected countries were hardly justifiable on sanitary grounds and that such an attitude proved injurious to general United States trade. Furthermore, they added, "economic protection in the guise of sanitary measures has been employed by foreign countries to the prejudice of our agricultural exports. We cannot consistently object to such measures abroad if we ourselves resort to them. . . ."[18]

Argentine technicians and veterinarians became aware of the growing probability of defeat of the proposed sanitary convention and urged the improvement of Argentine sanitary procedures for the betterment of livestock export potential. Such action, they thought, would take "from the enemies of Argentine commerce in meats" an argument that could have prejudicial consequences for the livestock industry. Groups in Britain, as well as in the United States, wished to cut Argentina out of domestic markets for fear of competition.[19]

As Franklin Roosevelt began his second term, the protectionist nature of the sanitary embargo became more apparent, and the sanitary convention was further away from ratification. Not only might live cattle introduce FMD, but also the millions of pounds of canned meat imported from South America now seemed a serious threat in the United States. The opposition continued, and the efforts of the State Department were of little avail.[20]

As livestock raisers in the United States continued in their opposition to the convention, the State Department attempted yet another maneuver to win support for the treaty. In an appeal to some sort of latent good sportsmanship on the part of the opposition, Hull peevishly characterized his opponents' attitude as "unwarranted and unfair." He pointed out that only Patagonian mutton would enter the United States. The *American Cattle Producer* retorted that Hull was confused and noted that the treaty failed to specify Patagonia and merely indicated any disease-free area. Even Espil was losing heart, for he clearly understood the political difficulty of obtaining a two-thirds vote favoring the treaty in the Senate.[21]

Meanwhile, Argentina began to take measures of her own in an attempt to win United States approval of the treaty. In October, 1937, the Argentine government decreed that movement of animals from FMD territories within the Argentine Republic was to be strictly regulated. This effort, however, failed to change official opinion in the United States, and by 1938 the only part of the United States government that remained passionately interested in the convention was the Division of American Republics in the State Department. In addition, other global affairs and the wavering domestic programs distracted Roosevelt, and he failed to exert further pressure in favor of the treaty.[22]

As the world moved closer to another global war that would eventually involve the entire hemisphere, the United States continued to feel the sting of some of its citizens' displeasure over suggestions to lift the embargo on Argentine meats. In 1939, Argentines were angered at another action of the United States: the refusal to allow Argentine meats to enter the United States for the restaurants at the World's Fair in that year. President Roberto Ortiz "fanned Argentine resentment against the United States by saying that . . . when [Argentina] asked for such a small thing as permission to bring in meat for the restaurants the American officials raised objections. . . ."

Ortiz further indicated that a few minor concessions, such as lowering the ban on meat, would immeasurably improve United States-Argentine trade relations. At the same time, he noted German willingness to purchase beef from the Platine Republic, although he failed to state that some German livestock was already infected. Further pressure came from the Argentine Embassy in the United States, which indicated that it believed the United States to be sincere when it negotiated the convention in 1935. The Embassy wondered why the United States maintained "old regulations based on no scientific considerations whatsoever, that are unnecessarily hindering our meat trade with the United States? . . ." According to the Argentine government, a total revision of United States regulations was required, based *"only and entirely* on the scientific safeguards for the prevention . . . of foot-and-mouth disease virus into the United States." [23]

Obviously rebuffed, Argentine public opinion turned upon United States business interests in Buenos Aires and made the conduct of business extremely difficult for United States companies in that city. Secretary Hull suggested that Section 306 (a) of the Smoot-Hawley tariff was partly responsible for the difficulties encountered by the United States businessmen in Argentina. Moreover, Argentina threatened to sever trade relations unless its meat was allowed entry into the United States. The *American Cattle Producer,* an excellent indicator of livestock raisers' opinion in the United States, pointed out that Argentina had failed to make any substantive attempt to eradicate FMD. Moreover, the journal contended, the beef purchased by Germany and England from Argentina accounted for recurrent FMD scourges in both of those countries. [24]

A proposal by President Roosevelt at a press conference in May, 1939, to purchase Argentine meat for use by United States military personnel, especially the Navy, was rebuffed by livestock raisers and congressmen. It was asked if the President would "drive the livestock producers to a state of peonage and peasantry in order to curry favor with an American Republic." The Roosevelt proposal met a sound legislative defeat when the Naval bill passed by Congress specifically prohibited the purchase of Argentine meat for use by the Navy while at sea. *El Comercio* of Lima, Peru, noted that such an action did not bode well for a government claiming to look for an improvement of trade relations with Latin America. The *Buenos Aires Herald* stated:

"The Argentine beef purchase, besides threatening to become a major political issue, is also expected to clarify the commercial aspects of the Good Neighbor Policy and to test the congressional willingness to yield minor trade concessions on behalf of Pan-Americanism." The United States did, however, make one concession: it allowed the importation of limited quantities of Argentine cooked beef for the New York World's Fair and the San Francisco Exposition under strictly regulated conditions. All trimmings from such meat had to be destroyed and not sold as hog swill because such use for feed on hog farms presented a high risk.[25]

The controversial Argentine-United States Sanitary Convention never even received hearings before the Senate Foreign Relations Committee, and in 1939, the State Department gave up all hope of ratification.[26] In the following year, at the Havana meeting of Foreign Ministers, where grave preoccupation existed over the impending hemispheric involvement in the war, sentiments of cooperation were formally expressed by the American republics. Espil wrote that "in accordance with the proposals for cooperation expressed at the Havana Conference, the Ministry of Agriculture has requested the Argentine Chancellery to take steps to secure the approval of the United States government of the Sanitary Convention." [27]

Espil's last effort failed along with those of United States proponents of the convention. Supporters of the treaty inside and outside the State Department, noting Argentine meat sales to Nazi Germany, argued that accepting meat from Argentina would keep authoritarianism out of the Americas by reducing Argentine dependence on German markets. Resolutions from various states, including Colorado, California, Texas, Illinois, Wyoming, and North Dakota, vigorously condemned the proposed convention and asked that it be withdrawn. The exigencies of war interrupted consideration of the pact. On April 8, 1948, President Harry S. Truman requested its withdrawal, and on April 17, a Senate resolution formally withdrew the convention from consideration. The failure of the United States to ratify the sanitary convention "demonstrated some of the limits of the Good Neighbor Policy . . . It was not possible," writes Bryce Wood, "to obtain the ratification of a Convention which was regarded by spokesmen of a politically powerful industry as harmful to their interests." [28]

Though the sanitary convention between the United States and

Argentina had, for all practical considerations, been defeated without so much as a hearing in the Senate Foreign Relations Committee, Argentina had taken further timid steps in an attempt to resolve the foot-and-mouth disease problem. By December, 1939, the *Instituto Nacional de la Fiebre Aftosa* (National Aftosa Institute) was created to carry on research and to publish findings about FMD. Work of the Institute was buttressed by private pharmaceutical houses carrying on independent research on aftosa vaccine.[29] In the following year, the Argentine government ordered a study by a commission to ascertain the most efficient way to eradicate the plague. These feeble steps, coupled with increasing Argentine neutrality in the global conflict, failed to ameliorate the already tense relations between Argentina and the United States.[30]

Some officials of the Argentine and United States governments, however, still sought ways to resolve the meat problem, and Argentina continually petitioned the State Department for a relaxation of sanitary regulations. Espil wrote in early 1941 that should the embargo be lifted, it seemed unlikely that lamb or mutton would enter the United States before 1942. Nevertheless, such action "at this time would have a very desirable psychological effect." Argentina continued aloof to United States efforts to improve relations and *La Nación* stated, "we cannot conceive of good neighborliness if the United States continues to condemn our meats on the grounds that they carry foot-and-mouth disease." That newspaper also condemned United States authorization to purchase Argentine corned beef for the Navy as a purely symbolic action, the quantity to be purchased being reduced substantially by Congressional action.[31]

Lend-lease, rationing, and growing meat shortages prompted the USDA to lift the embargo on mutton imports from Tierra del Fuego in June, 1941, after an extremely cautious decision was given by the Attorney General. Protests from United States cattlemen, however, quickly ensued. The Attorney General replied to inquiries from the State Department and the USDA that the Secretary of Agriculture was under no obligation to allow imports; existing regulations merely gave him defined discretionary powers if conditions, in his opinion, were acceptable for importation.[32] Prominent agriculturalists from the United States visited Argentina in that same month and recommended that the meat problem, the last obstacle to amicable relations, be resolved. Fundamentally, they proposed a completely independent study of the Patagonian problem. The United States Embassy in Buenos Aires noted, as of great significance, that one of the members of the group was the Secretary of the American National Livestock Association, which had so bitterly opposed the lifting of embargoes.[33]

Apparently motivated by the report rendered by the five agriculturalists, the USDA, on August 9 and 10, 1941, announced its desire to send its own investigation team to Tierra del Fuego for "political reasons." Reports from Argentina, however, showed that the announcement "produced a profoundly disturbing impression on Argentine public opinion and is being interpreted as our placing internal politics above what Argentina considers to be fair dealing." The USDA preferred not to rely on Argentine findings and indicated this preference by conducting its own investigation.[34]

With a somewhat qualified decision from the Attorney General about the classification of Tierra del Fuego, the USDA decided to send Dr. S. O. Fladness of the BAI to the area to investigate both the Chilean and Argentine portions of the island since, in the opinion of the Attorney General, they were inseparable.[35] Thus, in December, Fladness arrived in Argentina to determine if Tierra del Fuego was indeed free of FMD. He reported that he had found no evidence of aftosa in Tierra del Fuego at the time of his visit, and Argentina announced that it would sell 350,000 head of sheep to the United States from that region.[36] The Fladness report, however, failed to receive wide circulation because pressures coming primarily from United States livestock raisers and their Congressional spokesmen were exerted on the Secretary of Agriculture. Argentina demonstrated a decided coolness at the Rio Conference of 1942. The Secretary of Agriculture later reported he "was no longer satisfied" that the importation of meat from Tierra del Fuego would not risk the introduction of the disease into the United States.[37] Though no direct causal relation can be drawn between Argentina's attitude at Rio and the action of the Secretary of Agriculture, it is conceivable that the Argentine mood provided a convenient loophole by which mutton imports could be prohibited.

Caution on the part of the Secretary of Agriculture proved wise, for another extensive outbreak seized Argentina in 1942. Newspaper comment in the area avoided direct mention of the epizoötic and a "deliberate evasion or reference to and comment on the seriousness and extent of the outbreak" was reported. The outbreak began in the littoral province of Entre Ríos, and 1,545 infected premises were reported by July, 1942. By November, the number of cases declined, but animals continued to be shipped even if infected. "One veterinarian," reported the United States Embassy "referred to animals arriving in the Liniers Market 'on their knees.' " The intensity of the new infection was explained in part by the introduction of a different virus type, probably originating in Paraguay or Brazil.[38]

Argentina was critically aware of the problems posed both for her domestic economy and for her international commerce by the persistence of foot-and-mouth disease. An education campaign was initiated by the *Dirección de Sanidad Animal* with the dissemination of information about meat inspection, means of determining the presence of FMD, and measures to be taken against the malady.[39] By August, 1945, the Argentine government decreed the creation of the *Instituto para Elaborar Vacunas contra la Aftosa* (Institute for Development of Aftosa Vaccine) and an all-out fight against the disease was announced. Also, a decree ordered that all animals entering Patagonia from north of Neuquén and Río Negro were required to have FMD vaccinations.[40]

The Argentine aftosa problem also indirectly affected relations between Colombia and Venezuela, two countries at the time free of FMD. Colombia warned Venezuela that it would ban all Venezuelan cattle if Venezuela continued to purchase stock from FMD-infected Argentina. It was noted that many Colombian provinces imported great quantities of Venezuelan stock, and Colombia justifiably feared the inadvertent introduction of the malady.[41]

Uruguay

Though Argentina held the limelight during the Good Neighbor and war years, Uruguay, Brazil, Chile, Bolivia, and Peru also were forced to contend with aftosa and its concomitant problems. Uruguay, another country of the Río de la Plata region, voiced many of the same complaints that had been made by her southern neighbor.

As early as 1935, one Uruguayan newspaper noted that whenever a group of meat importers wished to curtail a country's purchase of meat, the threat of foot-and-mouth disease was suggested. Though some protests were raised against England, the United States bore the brunt of the criticism. It was charged that the United States continually sold more goods to South America in 1933 and 1934 than it purchased. "In its feverish Utopia it would insist even today, and in spite of the complete failure of its policy of tariffs and barriers," upon the increase of its exports by 100 per cent and the reduction of its imports to zero "as if selling without buying were possible." Uruguayan national interests, it was noted, lay in not "permitting the unjust discrediting of our products, the interest of the United States, and of all, lies in maintaining a cordial and sincere equilibrium, in order that Pan Americanism may not become a useless word, or something worse—a bad word." [42]

The Buenos Aires Conference in 1936 also gave Uruguay an opportunity to make its bid for entry into the United States meat market. Noting the way in which the Argentine Rural Society hoped to induce Roosevelt to purchase Argentine meat, *La Mañana* of Montevideo urged the Uruguayan delegation to press its case, noting that if Argentina was to be allowed entry of chilled meat under strict regulation, Uruguay should have the same privilege. Like Argentina, Uruguay also failed in its attempt, and *El Diario* condemned the United States for its failure to lift trade barriers. The newspaper, in addition, called United States tariffs "exaggerated agrarian protectionism," and damned United States officials who decried economic nationalism yet were its chief practitioners. [43]

During the same period when Argentina attempted to gain ratification of the sanitary convention, Uruguay made other attempts to gain entry into the United States beef market but met with the same failures as did Argentina. Even as hemispheric involvement in World War II increased and armed conflict broke out between the United States and the Axis powers, Uruguay hoped that exigencies of war would lead to a lowering of trade restrictions. Uruguayan hopes, however, were set back when Fladness reported an extremely serious outbreak of FMD in Uruguay in 1942. He requested that the Department of State ask its legation to inform the USDA periodically as to the development of FMD in Uruguay. [44] In response to these instructions, the Embassy at Montevideo reported that conditions in Uruguay were indeed serious. The Ministry of Husbandry and Agriculture kept few records of FMD outbreaks and the number of cases reported, and no attempts were made to classify the viruses. A report less than a year later indicated that the incidence of disease, though still severe, was diminishing. Nonetheless, the loss of cattle as a result of slaughter operations in an attempt to eradicate the disease was reported to have been in excess of two million dollars.[45]

Brazil

Brazil, as well as Uruguay and Argentina, had a new political regime that promised the amelioration of social ills, but the new regime failed to control, much less to eradicate, FMD. In fact, widespread FMD was reported throughout Pernambuco, Alagôas, Paraíba, and Rio Grande do Sul. Ceará, however, happily reported the eradication of the malady. By October, 1934, the disease became more intense in Pernambuco, and two years later the epizoötic reached disastrous proportions again in Pernambuco, Rio Grande do Norte, and Paraíba. Members of the Animal Sanitary Police were quickly dispatched in an attempt to eradicate the disease. Even though aftosa was rampant on Brazilian soil, the government of Getúlio Vargas made another attempt to ship Zebus to Mexico via New Orleans. The USDA, on the basis of BAI regulations, informed Brazil through the State Department that the Zebus could not stop at New Orleans.[46] By mid-1941 Brazilian FMD problems were still plaguing the country. Aftosa remained highly active, and little progress was made in immunization against the disease. Thus, Brazil in the depression and war years faced a formidable task on the home front against *la fiebre aftosa*.[47]

Chile, Bolivia, and Ecuador

On the other side of the Andes, Chile encountered much the same problem as her eastern neighbors. Restrictions ringed Chilean attempts to export animals and animal by-products to the United States. Even hay from Chile required the strictest of sanitary and quarantine controls. Yet, Chile persisted in its efforts, and in 1934, the Chilean Consul in Chicago requested copies of BAI regulations with a hint that Chile would like to export meat to the United States.[48] The USDA remained consistent, especially in view of developments in Chile. By 1936 reports of widespread aftosa in Chile reached the State Department. The Agricultural and Livestock Society of Osorio Province appealed directly to the Ministry of Agriculture for funds to fight the malady, and the direct and indirect damages paid to cattle owners amounted to $540,000. Six years later FMD had not abated, and one Chilean charlatan hoped to sell a magic formula to the USDA for aftosa eradication. By 1942, Chile still suffered from scattered outbreaks.[49]

The Chilean outbreaks were complicated by local milk dealers who, in violation of strict regulations in the cities and smaller towns, carried their milk on horse-drawn two-wheeled carts. Milk shortages existed in the large cities because of strict regulatory measures. In addition, when the first case of the disease was discovered in Los Andes, the Chilean terminus of the trans-Andean railroad from Argentina, cattle importations from Argentina were temporarily prohibited.[50] The situation was again aggravated in central Chile by Argentine imports. Over 450 premises were affected, and the Ministry of Agriculture ordered the immediate slaughter of all diseased cattle as well as stringent inspection at border stations. Again, the Andean passes connecting Chile and Argentina were closed to Argentine cattle. Chile thus demonstrated a willingness within its limited resources to fight FMD with the only then generally accepted weapon—slaughter of diseased and directly exposed stock.[51]

Livestock in Bolivia also suffered from FMD during the war years. Reports from the Departments of Tarija and Santa Cruz indicated a highly virulent aftosa epidemic. Bolivian veterinarians lacked the materials with which to combat the malady, and officials laid the blame on careless customs inspection at the Bolivian-Argentine border. Moreover, careless inspection at slaughterhouses clearly contributed to the spread of the disease. Though all cattle slaughtered in La Paz were required to have health certificates, it was "admitted that cattle infected with aphthous fever and for which health certificates were issued, have been slaughtered at the local slaughterhouse." [52]

Ecuador noted the appearance of a rapidly spreading vesicular disease in 1943. The malady was concentrated in the eastern provinces but spread with rapidity to the ranches in the Sierras. At this point, a positive diagnosis of aftosa was not made.[53]

Thus, in a period of twelve years (1933–1945), FMD increased its strangling hold on Latin America and forced the affected countries to a reduced trade potential. As reprehensible as some may find the protectionist policy of the United States during this time, it nonetheless kept that country free of aftosa. Obviously, both sanitary and economic considerations served as rationale for the tariff barriers imposed to protect the United States from South American livestock. During the depression and the war years FMD failed to become a legitimate threat to the United States national interest. The proposed sanitary convention of 1935 would have been a greater benefit to Argentina than to the United States. Argentina stood to gain a market for its livestock and livestock products, while the United States risked the introduction of FMD had the convention been ratified. After the war, Mexico posed a much more serious threat to United States livestock interests, for *fiebre aftosa* struck in December, 1946, and the United States found itself fighting along with Mexico to protect a vital industry.

CHAPTER III

THE MEXICAN EXPERIENCE I

The United States-Mexican Sanitary Convention of 1928 was observed more in the breach than in the practice, for both countries violated the agreement in the 1930's and 1940's. Both parties affirmed their mutual cooperation in livestock disease control at the meeting of the Mexican-United States Agricultural Commission in Mexico City in 1944. Mutual effort was compromised, however, for in October, 1945, Mexico, with apparent knowledge of the United States, imported 120 Zebu bulls from Brazil with no retaliatory embargo by the United States. In addition, one Texas breeder also brought in Zebus via Mexico without a reported word of complaint from his government.[1] The importation of Brazilian bulls into either Mexico or the United States created a serious problem, for Texas breeders apparently planned to use their Zebus in Mexico as breeding stock to sell to Mexicans as well as to other North Americans. Mexico chose to purchase its stock directly. According to Mexican Secretary of Agriculture Marte R. Gómez, a year later Brazil again attempted to export Zebu bulls to Mexico, but at this point Gómez refused permission for the entry of the animals. Pressures were brought to bear on Gómez by President Manuel Ávila Camacho, and the Secretary relented but only allowed the landing of 327 Zebus on Isla de Sacrificios off the coast of Veracruz, which was intended to be a location of precautionary inspection and quarantine.[2]

When the cattle arrived, they were quarantined aboard ship because Gómez ordered a series of tests meant to safeguard his country from a possible FMD epidemic. At the same time, the United States, which previously had acted as observer and advisor, took action and placed an embargo on all Mexican stock entering the United States. The blow to the economy of northern Mexico was catastrophic. During the war up to this point Mexican cattlemen had sold as many as 500,000 head of cattle annually to the United States. This lucrative market was lost through the newly imposed embargo. Mexico immediately began to negotiate with the United States for a removal of the embargo through the Secretariat of Foreign Relations under Dr. Francisco Castillo Nájera as well as through the Mexican delegation to the meeting of the Mexican-United States Agricultural Commission, which met in the summer of 1946. The United States government's attitude remained firm; Mexico, if it wanted the embargo lifted, would have to rid itself of the bulls. During the meeting, however, the United States delegates agreed to permitting a series of observations and tests by a Mexican-United States team of veterinarians. If these proved negative, lifting of the quarantine was considered possible.[3]

When the bulls finally debarked on August 31, investigations began immediately, and, after a long series of tests, the bulls were considered to be free of evidence of contagion. Gómez reported, however, that he maintained a skeptical attitude and ordered that the animals "remain completely localized and isolated, with no contact with other cattle than those placed as detectors in the observation pastures." Finally, the animals were landed on the mainland on September 24, and President Harry S. Truman lifted the embargo on Mexican stock. Gómez, however, refused to yield to the "deceitful exhilaration" that prevailed, and warned that any movement of the bulls would result in rather stiff fines.[4]

The Zebu bulls caused a furor in Mexico. Gómez accused Guillermo Quesada Bravo, former Director of Husbandry, of acting as the agent for Brazilians who hoped to use Mexico as a way station to sell their stock to Texas breeders. Quesada Bravo, on the other hand, alleged that Gómez, in an attempt to cover up his own complicity in the matter, used political character assassination to destroy his career. Mexican newspapers and cattlemen's associations soon became extremely partisan, and vitriolic polemics spread across the pages of Mexico City journals. Ultimately, Gómez won out. He was staunchly supported by the cattlemen's associations, and he had at his disposal the resources of the government.[5]

By December, 1946, a new regime came into power, and Miguel Alemán Valdés, the new president, appointed Narzario S. Ortiz Garza as Gómez' successor. Gómez, in a brief to Ortiz Garza, outlined the difficulties encountered with the bulls and the incipient danger of FMD. He wrote, "the danger of foot-and-mouth disease is real, and in case of erring, better through excess of caution than for lack of it." [6]

United States officials remained ostensibly aloof from the political wrangling that occurred in Mexico during the conflict between Gómez and Quesada Bravo, though they might be judged by some as culpable for a lack of official firmness about the bulls. At a time when United States relations in Latin America were at a low ebb, an attempt was made through reluctant acceptance of tacit modifications of quarantine requirements vis-à-vis the Brazilian Zebus to moderate the complicated situation. Considering Brazilian public opinion as well as judgment about sanitary requirements at the time, the possible alternative of dumping the bulls into the Gulf of Mexico would have spelled disaster for United States-Brazilian relations.[7]

La fiebre aftosa (Type A) soon struck Mexico, and by late October, 1946, the area where the bulls had debarked in Veracruz was infected. Within less than a month the *Municipio* (county) of Boca del Río, Veracruz, reported 300 head of infected cattle. Confusion reigned, and the disease spread. According to Dr. Fernando Camargo Núñez, many cattle raisers thought the disease to be vesicular stomatitis or *mal de la yerba*. Preliminary positive diagnosis of FMD by Drs. Fernando Camargo Núñez and José Figueroa was buttressed by confirmatory diagnoses by USDA veterinarians, and Mexico was officially declared to be infected with aftosa. On December 26, the United States closed its borders to Mexican livestock and livestock products. Large, alarming headlines announced the closure of the border, and FMD relentlessly pushed into the Federal District and the states of Veracruz, México, Tlaxcala, and Puebla. Within a month, seventeen states, including 57 million hectares of Mexico's agricultural land and 15 million cattle, hogs, sheep, and goats were in the infected zone. As in Chile, the problem was intensified through the movement of *campesinos* over the hills and mountains with little, if any, regard for a quarantine that they did not understand.[8]

By mid-January, 1947, at least 35,000 head of infected cattle existed in Mexico; yet, Secretary of Agriculture Ortiz Garza stated optimistically that "the crisis could be considered past if taken into account that there exist in Mexico ten million head of cattle."[9] The disease, however, continued to spread, and the Mexican government began its anti-aftosa operations with very little technical experience. The most efficient method of eradication known at the time was inspection, slaughter of infected and exposed stock, deep burial, and rigid disinfection and quarantine, known in Mexico as the Alemán-Ortiz Garza plan.[10] Though one critic damned the slowness of Mexican bureaucracy for the rapid spread of the disease, a functioning National Commission to Combat Aftosa was formed in January, 1947, and it undertook the drastic eradication measures called for in the Alemán-Ortiz Garza plan.[11] The Mexican Army provided quarantine stations, transportation, and police control for the sanitary brigades, and local *juntas municipales* (municipal directorates) and regional cattlemen's organizations in the affected area gave immediate promises of support to the National Commission.[12]

Aftosa to the Mexican *campesino* was an almost unknown phenomenon, and officials and technicians groped for a means by which the *campesino* might be made to understand the necessity of the severe measures necessary to eradicate the disease. The state committees and the *juntas municipales* joined the Director of Husbandry, Dr. José Figueroa, in the distribution of over 200,000 propaganda items. At the same time, the United States' involvement began with the closure of the border in December, 1946, and Dr. Fernando Camargo related that he flew to Washington with Oscar Flores, Undersecretary of Animal Husbandry, to negotiate for United States aid. Moreover, inter-American cooperation made itself evident when United States, Chilean, Brazilian, and Argentine scientists joined Mexico in its attempts to rid that country of FMD.[13]

United States livestockmen favored aid to Mexico because the FMD threat presented a real and present danger to their own interests. Congress rushed through a bill authorizing the Secretary of Agriculture to give aid to Mexico in order to protect vital United States interests. By March 1, President Truman signed the bill into a law, and the USDA, along with the State Department and the Mexican Secretariat of Foreign Relations, began developing a program for aid to Mexico. On March 6, the Mexican-United States Agricultural Commission met and agreed on a mutually acceptable program. Their recommendations included the creation of a joint commission based in Mexico City with a Mexican director and a United States co-director, with each section of the commission to be composed of three members from each country and an unlimited number of advisors. Compensation for slaughtered stock was divided between the two countries, with the United States to pay for cattle (*ganado mayor*) and Mexico to pay for sheep, goats, and hogs (*ganado menor*). Additionally, Mexico supplied the laborers, and veterinarians of the two nations worked side by side. The United States provided most of the technicians and equipment. The Mexican military was given complete police power in enforcement of Commission requirements. Thus, on March 18, 1947, an agreement between Mexico and the United States established financial, administrative, and procedural ground rules, and on April 1, the Comisión México-Americana para la Erradicación de la Fiebre Aftosa (CMAPEFA) began to function.[14]

CMAPEFA entered the battle against aftosa with determined vigor under the direction of Oscar Flores, Subsecretary of Husbandry, and Dr. Maurice S. Shahan of the BAI. Flores remained as director until the end of the campaign in 1954, but the United States changed its co-directors with some frequency, appointing General Harry H. Johnson in 1948 and after May, 1951, replacing him with Dr. Leroy R. Noyes. Mexico was divided into zones, described as "infected," "buffer," and "clean," and all animal transportation became subject to strict quarantine regulations under the direction of Commission veterinarians. Additionally, animals within an infected zone could not move to other regions, and products of livestock in the afflicted area were refused transport out of the zone.[15]

Aftosa seriously upset Mexico's economy and society, requiring a long period of adaptation. The United States, however, allowed its borders to stay open to tourist traffic and to non-livestock commerce in an attempt to ameliorate the economic dislocation that aftosa imposed on Mexico. The otherwise closed border, nonetheless, rendered a severe blow to cattle producers, primarily those in Sonora, Chihuahua, and Coahuila. These three states lost an export potential of 304,793 head of cattle valued at 32,417,365 pesos annually. Additionally, the slaughter operations undercut the campesinos' meat and milk supplies as well as those of the metropolitan inhabitants. In addition to meat and milk shortages caused by slaughter, shysters and prostitutes quickly separated the *campesino* from the money he received in compensation for his stock. Finally, oxen constituted the principal work animal, and eradication measures rapidly decimated the oxen supply, causing a serious corn crop failure in the first year of the campaign.[16] In less than a year, CMAPEFA, despite opposition by the United States, was forced to change from a slaughter program, the only sure method of eradication, to a modified slaughter-vaccine approach in an attempt to save the rural economy.

Equitable compensation proved a problem for CMAPEFA, and before the creation of that body the National Commission found itself without sufficient funds for adequately compensating the livestock raisers.[17] Minimum compensation standards were established, but bureaucratic snarls involving the provision of funds hindered efficient operation. Finally, joint handling of funds was decided upon, with the United States paying the bulk of the compensations. Along with the monetary compensation given the peasants, the USDA, along with ranchers in FMD-free Mexico, supplied tractors, horses, and mules to the infected regions for use as draft stock.[18] The peasants, however, failed to appreciate mules and their idiosyncracies:

> . . . They [the Mexican peasants] learned that the mule was an animal without patience. Beat him and curse him, and the beast fought back. He kicked and he bit. He took fright at all manner of foolish things and wrecked harnesses and plows. And even when he was willing to follow the furrow, he walked too fast.

Ay! How one did pant, trying to keep up with the seedless beasts! How the sweat did pour! How one's legs did ache! How one did long for the slow, patient gait of the oxen—the gait of México.[19]

Cattle that remained in the infected region but were not directly exposed to FMD presented another problem that was joined by a growing milk shortage in Mexico City. One solution was the movement of cattle into central Mexico in an attempt to allay a critical situation. Salvage operations, under the auspices of the National Commission and with the cooperation of CMAPEFA, also began, though they were criticized by both the United States Congress and Mexico City newspapers.[20] These operations failed to resolve a meat shortage in the afflicted zone, and San Luis Potosí, for example, complained of shortages because of the amount of paperwork required to move livestock to market.[21]

Salvage operations in the infected and buffer zones failed, however, to alleviate the potential ruin of northern Mexico. The damming-up of cattle in the northern states led by December, 1947, to plans for cannery construction in the North. By this means, potentially infected meat could be rendered safe. Though the prices paid for the canned meat were only about half of that formerly received in the United States, *norteño* cattlemen preferred these prices to ruination. In 1948, the USDA negotiated contracts for 73 million pounds of canned meat, and by 1951, the United States had purchased 218 million pounds of canned meat, 150 million pounds of which were sold to European countries. Moreover, in 1949, the USDA noted that Mexico's inspection service had so improved that salt-cured meat was allowed entry under rigorous supervision into the United States from northern Mexico. These cooperative efforts removed the stigma from the closed border, which no longer symbolized Yankee stubbornness.[22]

During the initial phases of the joint operation, CMAPEFA faced supply problems, such as lack of heavy machinery for digging burial fossas, tractors, and laboratory equipment. Much of this essential matériel soon came from the United States.[23] As the campaign developed, additional storage facilities were needed, and warehouse construction began at San Jacinto, D.F., the headquarters of the Dirección General de Investigaciones Pecuarias (General Directorate of Agricultural Research), and in provincial areas, such as Zacatecas, San Luis Potosí, and Guadalajara.[24]

President Miguel Alemán contributed personally to the campaign against FMD. On June 6, 7, and 8, 1947, he traveled through the states of Querétaro, México, and Guanajuato to gain personal support for the eradication measures undertaken by CMAPEFA. In the main, his trip proved a success, though complaints continued about the slowness of indemnity payments, and some *campesinos* insisted in the belief that FMD did not exist in Mexico. As a result, they fell prey to charlatans peddling magic elixirs, which in turn deterred eradication and contributed to the spread of the malady.[25]

Despite CMAPEFA's efforts, the spread of aftosa continued, and by June, 1947, it was estimated that an additional 500,000 head of livestock should be destroyed for effective eradication. Cattlemen began to ask for vaccine as a control measure, and the Ministry of Agriculture dispatched envoys to explain that slaughter still remained the most effective method of eradication, which was the Commission's goal. The campaign slowed in September, 1947, when the *fiestas patrias* (Mexico's Independence Day, September 16) pulled Army contingents away from quarantine stations for duty in parades and in the cities. Mexican regional *políticos,* including the governors of Oaxaca, Guanajuato, Guerrero, Hidalgo, Jalisco, Michoacán, Morelos, Puebla, Querétaro, Tlaxcala, Veracruz, and the Federal District, their *presidentes municipales,* and other local officials, met and declared their full support for CMAPEFA efforts.[26]

Mexico also faced a closed border to the south. Guatemala increased border patrol activities and charged that the United States was more interested in eradicating infection in those areas closest to its own borders than in concentrating on Veracruz and areas farther south. Yet, Guatemalan complaints to the contrary notwithstanding, Chiapas, Aguascalientes, Zacatecas, and San Luis Potosí were declared free of infection, and Oaxaca contained only small loci of infection. Control animals were introduced into the area to assure the efficacy of disinfection, and cattle from the clean zone were imported to restock the area.[27]

Progress in the first year of the campaign was checkered, but substantive advances were made in the eradication process. Bureaucratic sluggishness and the subjective nature of Mexican politics, according to Dr. M. R. Clarkson, accounted in part for the initial slowness of the campaign. He declared:

> The Central Government was what is to me a rather un-fathomable arrangement with the governors of the various states. In many ways, they seem to have full power, and in others ways they seem helpless, and the governors of the states can control their people independently of the principal Government.

Some United States congressmen indicated indignation over Mexico's political complexities and urged that the mess be straightened out. General Charles Corlett, special advisor to the Secretary of Agriculture, stated, however, that the reformation could not be made abruptly:

> You have got to be very patient with them. At the conferences we attended they don't delegate authority. . . . We also know of instances of where the governor has let the Presidente down, and you are going to run into those things all the time. It is a thing requiring great patience.[28]

Mexico and the United States made a unique scientific contribution to the eradication of foot-and-mouth disease, for, as the first year of the campaign closed, outright total slaughter was abandoned. Its replacement by a combined slaughter-vaccination program necessitated an amendment of the agreement that bound Mexico and the United States together because experimentation with live viruses had been specifically prohibited, as had vaccine. The amending process merely required action by the Secretaries of Agriculture, and plans soon began for a vaccine-producing laboratory in Mexico. Both countries still maintained that the most efficacious method was slaughter, and the United States adamantly contended that any other technique was still unproved. Yet fear of being asked by Mexico to withdraw and the latent threat implicit in such a withdrawal forced the United States to acquiesce in demands from the Mexican countryside for vaccine. Vaccination, then, entailed giving "all susceptible animals in the affected area" temporary immunization that would starve the virus for lack of targets.[29]

Problems of production and procurement of adequate vaccine initially caused difficulties, and CMAPEFA was forced to look abroad for assistance. England sent advisors, and vaccines arrived from Holland, Switzerland, Argentina, and Denmark. Mexican scientists also visited England and South America, and experimentation began even before the slaughter operations terminated. By January, 1948, vaccine production embarked on a high-risk course. CMAPEFA Co-Director Oscar Flores told Mexican scientists that they symbolized the hopes of the Mexican people. "In your hands we confide the success of the campaign." A *Consejo Consultivo* (Consultative Council) was formed under Fernando Camargo to regulate the flow of foreign vaccine into Mexico.[30]

With the creation of a technical and administrative mechanism to undertake the task of developing a suitable vaccine, and keeping Mexico from becoming a dumping ground for foreign biologicals of unknown or questionable efficacy, an expansion of facilities was needed. The handling of live virus was dangerous, and a safe location was necessary to limit insofar as possible new outbreaks in and around the Federal District. Two additional locations, aside from San Jacinto, were located and made ready to receive experimental livestock from northern FMD-free states.[31]

By May, 1948, vaccine production in Mexico was sufficient to allow the cessation of vaccine imports from abroad. Vaccination began in selected areas under close inspection, but production was slowed at first because of limited facilities for testing and storage of vaccine. Space limitations notwithstanding, production by October, 1948, increased to the point that by the end of the month one million doses were ready for use in the field, and by the end of January, 1949, the monthly production had doubled.[32]

The great need for vaccine production forced CMAPEFA to look for still more facilities. Ultimately, Palo Alto, D.F., thirteen kilometers north of Mexico City on the México-Toluca Highway was selected as the site. Invitations were sent to dignitaries from the United States, Europe, and South America for the inauguration of the newly built facility on September 1, 1949. Dr. P. V. Cardon, Research Administrator of the USDA, warned that a long, arduous task remained in " 'starving out the virus.' " He noted, however, that as technicians began in the new surroundings, they became " 'part of a never-ending pattern in which science is pitted against the ills that beset mankind.' " Mexico and the United States were proud, he declared, in being part of " 'that pattern as we dedicate this laboratory today. At the same time, we rededicate ourselves to the job of wiping out foot-and-mouth disease in Mexico.' " The new facility gave CMAPEFA a laboratory comparable with those in Pirbright, England, and elsewhere in the world, and facilitated virus identification, improved typification, and made distinction between FMD and vesicular stomatitis more readily available. However, the exigencies of the campaign did not allow for the transfer of vaccine production and testing facilities from San Jacinto and San Angel to Palo Alto. Production continued at San Jacinto, and virus typification and testing were carried on at Palo Alto.[33]

Production of the vital vaccine continued at a rapid pace. By the end of 1950, 53,524,000 doses of vaccine came from Commission laboratories. In 1948, 1949, and 1950, 15 million head of livestock (including sheep, goats, and pigs) received 60,054,962 doses, the objective being three vaccinations a year at intervals of three to four months. Yet, vaccine production and vaccination of susceptible stock met with technical problems, such as testing for innocuity and potency, and dosage. Once stabilized through rigid testing procedures in the laboratory and in the field, production became a mathematical process. Palo Alto was to become the headquarters of the General Directorate of Agricultural Research, with expanded functions beyond the study of vesicular viruses. Artificial insemination, begun at Palo Alto during the last year of the anti-aftosa campaign, continues. Animals were imported in 1951, and breed improvement projects initiated the rehabilitation of the depleted livestock industry in central Mexico through artificial insemination. Also, tests on feeds and animal diets are conducted at Palo Alto, as well as production of vaccine for *Derriengue* (paralytic bat-borne rabies). The Comisión México-Americana para la Prevención de la Fiebre Aftosa (CMAPPFA) now maintains laboratory facilities at Palo Alto to conduct tests for stomatitis and suspected FMD outbreaks.[34]

Thus the first year of the anti-aftosa campaign in Mexico saw the introduction of a highly problematical approach to eradication—vaccination and limited slaughter. Yet, without this compromise, the ruin of the agrarian economy was imminent. The creation and development of vaccine-producing facilities contributed significantly to Mexican needs in the rehabilitation of its livestock industry, and a steady improvement in the quality of stock in central Mexico became evident.

Moreover, the United States, forced to cope with Mexican conditions, proved itself adaptable. Its interest was threatened, and it responded in a way that ultimately strengthened United States-Mexican relations. Nearly a decade was required, however, before Mexico was totally freed of the viral menace.

CHAPTER IV

THE MEXICAN EXPERIENCE II

Aftosa failed to abate in Mexico by 1948, and, in the opinion of some observers, became increasingly pronounced as a result of the new, experimental vaccination program. Congress, yielding to pressures from livestock interests in the United States, viewed the new program with skepticism, and predicted that eradication was further away than before the cooperative venture began.[1] With the change in program, increased border patrol activities began along the international boundary to remove stray animals that wandered from Mexico into the Southwest. Inspection programs were also initiated at all ports of entry because commerce and air traffic from Mexico constituted a threat to the United States. Aftosa, being caused by a virus that is easily transported, required increased vigilance in Mexico, and disinfection tanks were built along main Mexican highways.[2]

The vaccination campaign did not, however, preclude slaughter of livestock in isolated outbreaks. The State of Tabasco, for instance, offered a "magnificent example" of the use of slaughter techniques in the future.[3] Yet, vaccine production continued, and strenuous efforts were made to revaccinate livestock to ensure the starvation of the virus. The Mexican *campesino,* however, frequently failed to comprehend that the vaccine was effective only temporarily and that it needed periodic readministration.[4]

Outstanding successes were not achieved in 1948, though some signs pointed to a more favorable situation in 1949. Increased efforts in disseminating information won the support of the *Sinarquistas* (a conservative political party), whose large rural following added to the growing lists of CMAPEFA supporters.[5] Moreover, a rigorous inspection policy showed that by March, 1949, over three million head of stock, approximately one-third of the total in the affected area, had been inspected. These and increased surveillance of transport facilities added ultimately to the control of the malady.[6]

In May, 1949, the disease struck 384 miles south of Brownsville, Texas, and CMAPEFA feared that aftosa might sweep north and endanger the United States even more. Although the outbreak was rapidly eradicated, the event led BAI officials to emphasize the

> insidious nature of foot-and-mouth disease. In spite of experiencing 29 days without evidence of active infection, this turn of events indicates the severity of the disease and the possibility of its sudden reappearance. Need for continual vigilance and precautions is apparent . . . if the plans for control and final eradication are to be successful.[7]

An outbreak in October, 1949, threatened to change the whole complexion of the anti-FMD campaign, for a new viral type, Type "O," made its appearance. Rapid eradication and disinfection curtailed further outbreaks, and it was announced that slaughter would again be used if Type O should reappear. The effectiveness with which CMAPEFA met the new challenge "convinced many of the program's severest critics that the efficiency and thoroughness of the organization was equal to any task which might arise." The new virus was declared eradicated by February, 1950.[8]

The prognosis for 1950 was more cheerful, and by February, vaccination efforts seemed to have been successful when no outbreaks were reported. The following month, a cutback in vaccination was announced, and CMAPEFA declared that it would put even greater emphasis on inspection. Incipient successes brought concomitant dangers of over-confidence and complacency among the Mexican people. Mexican livestock raisers, however, feared that the vaccine cutback endangered their interests, and the Asociación Nacional de Productores de Leche Pura, for example, noted that the new Palo Alto laboratory was not fulfilling its function. Moreover, they stated that a reappearance of aftosa meant that slaughter, not vaccine, would be used as the combative method.[9] But setbacks and technical difficulties were finally overcome. The last known infection was eliminated in August, 1951, and on September 1, 1952, Mexico was declared free of aftosa. Accordingly, the United States reopened its borders to Mexican livestock. At this time, CMAPEFA dropped the word "eradication" from its name and became the *Comisión México-Americana para la Prevención de la Fiebre Aftosa,* or CMAPPFA.[10]

Yet, the conquest of the virus proved to have been only temporary, for CMAPPFA announced an outbreak in Gutiérrez Zamora, Veracruz, in May, 1953. The United States border was again closed and the already established facilities in Mexico again were operated. The same stringent sanitary measures were applied, and a military cordon isolated the area.[11]

The new control procedures proved effective. By March, 1954, the last known pocket of infection was declared eradicated, and control animals were introduced into the area. Two months later, Mexico was again declared free of aftosa.[12] The diligent efforts of CMAPEFA and CMAPPFA had borne fruit.

The final success, however, had been marred by persistent superstition, ignorance, greed, and gullibility that had acted as destructive forces and had made the efforts of the Joint Commission more difficult. Even though the vast majority of the Mexican people supported the efforts of CMAPEFA, opposition from an intransigent minority began even before the United States officially gave help to Mexico. The slaughter campaign had a profound effect on the sentimental Mexican peasant who considered his few head of stock as a part of his family.[13] The principal areas of opposition were Guerrero, Michoacán, and state of México, and in June, 1947, CMAPEFA temporarily pulled its forces out of Guerrero because of relentless opposition. Within less than six months, the same thing would occur in Michoacán.[14] Less sophisticated cattle raisers failed to understand the necessity of slaughter as a means of eradicating FMD. Even the governor of Tlaxcala, for example, stated that with Tlaxcala's 20,000 head of cattle, only 10 per cent were slaughtered, and he implied that slaughter was unessential to eradication.[15] Gossip and half-truths acted as stimuli for the opposition, and avaricious cattle buyers often told peasants that CMAPEFA brigades paid nothing for the stock. Also, according to one report, peasants were informed that Joint Commission personnel would castrate all the old men of the village if they did not cooperate. With the initiation of vaccination, "Yankee-phobes" in Mexico declared that eating meat from vaccinated stock rendered the people sterile. This nefarious "fact" was said to constitute part of a "sinister plot of the United States to depopulate Mexico." [16]

Even religion played a part in the opposition to the anti-aftosa efforts. Rural Mexican religion, a combination of Old World faith and New World paganism, attributes much to Holy Days, Saints' Days, and other religious festivals. This form of veneration led to an unusual situation in Guerrero when peasants refused to corral their stock for vaccination and inspection. They stated that the animals were corraled but once a year, on October 18, San Lucas' Day. Therefore, with the support of the Mexican Army, the brigades were forced to capture, inspect, and vaccinate the cattle at different water holes.[17]

Moreover, the presence of military and occasional Army ineptitude engendered fear that hindered the progress of the campaign. One soldier stationed with a quarantine and inspection unit near Guadalajara reported that the people blamed the government for the supposedly low payments they received for slaughtered stock and on one occasion attempted to shoot him and other soldiers because they had done the actual slaughtering.[18]

Opposition to the campaign had its violent manifestations, often led by petty demagogues who opposed United States participation in the joint effort. In June, 1947, one Mexican veterinarian was killed because the peasants opposed the slaughter of livestock.[19] Three months later another Mexican veterinarian and six soldiers met their deaths at Senguio, Michoacán. Drunken peasants hacked up the seven men with machetes. The massacre led to temporary suspension of field operations, strengthening of military forces in Michoacán, and an increased education program. Some residents of Senguio opposed the participation of the United States, even though cattle in and around Senguio had not been slaughtered. The incident also had political repercussions because the ruling *Partido Revolucionario Institucional* (*PRI*) claimed the *Sinarquistas* were responsible for instigating the massacre. The latter, in return, accused the *PRI* of attempting to discredit a party that threatened the hegemony of the *PRI* in Mexico. Speedy action caused comment in Mexico, for many crimes remained outstanding while, according to *Excelsior,* rapid execution of justice came to the Indians of Senguio. Finally, one hundred persons were arrested for the massacre, and prison sentences were given as punishment.[20]

One of the greatest examples of the gullibility of the *campesinos* occurred on January 31, 1949, when Robert Proctor, a twenty-two year old livestock inspector from Tucson, Arizona, was killed at Temascalcingo, State of México. Hundreds of drunken peasants rushed Proctor's brigade. All but Proctor escaped, and he was handed over to drunken Indian women who proceeded to kill him with knives. Mexican officials quickly investigated and made arrests. The prosecution asked for capital punishment, and *Excelsior* reported that death sentences were given to twenty-eight persons. At the same time, the United States officials both in Mexico and the United States commented favorably on the cooperation and efficiency of the Mexican authorities.[21]

Opposition to participation of the United States began early, and many organized cattlemen's groups complained bitterly. One delegation from Michoacán told President Alemán that he should be cognizant of the "true feelings of the public which says that the campaign that extinguishes agricultural wealth is dictated by the United States government," which could not afford to have aftosa on its soil and "does not vacillate in condemning the nation [Mexico] to misery." Moreover, they added, the Good Neighbor Policy was dead because a good neighbor does not destroy another's economy.[22]

Demonstrations against the United States occasionally had violent overtones, and some Mexico City journals began to print anti-Yankee complaints. One poem in *Excelsior,* for example, excoriated the United States for acting in its own interests:

"Más Vale Tarde . . .
Cualquier res aftosa cura [el rifle sanitario]
y ya no se vuelva a enfermarse
de dicho mal se asegura
quién no puede equivocarse.

Y ahora en México se ve
como una triste verdad
¡qué ha sido peor el remedio
que la enfermedad!

Se mata sin compasión
nuestro ganado bovino
sólo para la protección
del ganado del vecino

Si la aftosa cunde allá
el vecino ganadero
de seguro perderá
mientras la ataca, dinero.

Y si allá no cunde, entiende
que esa gente, bien pagada
se hará más rica vendiendo
cueros, y leche enlatada.

Así, si el vecino ayuda
solo lo hace por su bien
y surge al pueblo una duda
¿quién está ayudando a quien?

Por eso, si éxito alcanza
aquella vacuna exótica
el suspender la matanza
será un labor patriótica.

Y aunque algo tarde empieza
¡aún será cosa oportuna
defender nuestra riqueza vacuna
con vacuna! [23]

Even temporary cessation of slaughter failed to stifle opposition, for if a vaccinated animal died, demagogues blamed the United States vaccine, even though only Mexican veterinarians and vaccinators administered the biologic. Moreover, the deep-seated animosity toward the United States led many people to prefer aftosa to United States activity in Mexico. Many acts of violence, moreover, were performed in an attempt to embarrass the United States.[24]

Mexico's political style perplexed the United States contingent of CMAPEFA because the power of *caciques* (bosses) and *caciquismo* (bossism) was blatant and unfamiliar.[25] If convinced that the anti-aftosa campaign would benefit them, the local *caciques* cooperated; if not, they led their followers into opposition. It became necessary, therefore, to expedite municipal progress through the *caciques*. Also, the tenuous allegiance existing between state governors and local officials dictated the amount of pressure for cooperation that the former could bring to bear on the latter.[26]

Although the Mexican political system is essentially dominated by one party, the *PRI,* provision exists for opposition parties, provided they do not threaten *PRI* control of the country. Delegates of one of the parties, the *Partido de Acción Nacional (PAN)*, planned a visit to Mexico City from La Piedad, Michoacán, to complain about electoral irregularities. The trip was cancelled by *PRI* officials, assertedly because of the danger of spreading aftosa. Another *PAN* group in Michoacán found that a meeting was cancelled, again for fear of spreading aftosa. Members of *PAN,* reported *Excelsior,* refrained from gathering, for they feared that "perhaps the 'sanitary rifle' would be used on them." [27]

In an attempt to quell opposition, Secretary of Agriculture Ortiz Garza announced in January, 1947, that aftosa would soon be defeated.[28] The Mexican Army, however, appraised the situation more realistically and ordered all military personnel to act as media agents for distributing information on aftosa and the means used to eradicate it.[29] After the Senguio massacre, CMAPEFA appointed *informadores,* or information men, for this task. These men, many of whom spoke the Indian languages and dialects, were dispatched into hostile areas to explain in detail the methods and rationale of eradicating and controlling FMD. In cases where information men could not speak the Indian dialects, trouble usually ensued, including violence.[30]

Early in the campaign, President Alemán himself appealed for help from the citizenry. On a trip to the Bajío region he underwent disinfection procedures as an example to a reluctant peasantry. Despite an intransigent minority of *caciques,* local political groups usually cooperated, and Commission brigades used them to gain *campesino* support. Added to this were cattlemen's groups, which were helpful in the recruitment of field personnel for local operations.[31]

With increased publicity efforts, especially after the Senguio incident, by mid-1949 opposition was appreciably reduced. A film was made for propaganda purposes and by October, 1947, was being shown in theaters around Toluca.[32] The cooperation of field personnel in dispelling fear also helped break down latent opposition, and radio and newspapers were somewhat useful in reaching the people. But because some newspapers became alarmist, official brochures were used increasingly. One such brochure explained in detail the advantage of vaccination:

> *CAMPESINO*
> Lee con atención este folleto para que conozca la verdad de como se hace y se prueba la vacuna que salvará a tus animales de la terrible fiebre aftosa.
>
> La vacuna es preparada con el mayor cuidado por médicos y hombres de ciencia que luchan para acabar con la fiebra aftosa. *ES MENTIRA* que la vacuna haga mal a los animales. *NO CREAS* a quienes tratan de engañarte y ayuda a las brigadas de vacunación dando facilidades para que tus animales sean vacunados.
>
> *ES POR MEXICO,* tu patria, que tienes la obligación de vacunar a tus animales y ayudar a los vacunadores. *SOLO CON LA VACUNA* se ayudará a salvar a tu ganado. La vacuna y que tus animales sean vacunados no te costará ni un centavo . . .
>
> . . . te aseguramos que la vacuna contra la fiebre aftosa NO ENFLAQUECE AL GANADO, NO LO INUTILIZA PARA QUE PUEDA REPRODUCIRSE, NO OCASIONA

LOS ABORTOS, NO ES DAÑINA PARA TUS ANIMALES Y SOBRE TODO NO TE CUESTA NI UN SOLO CENTAVO.[33]

Mexican schools and the Mexican clergy joined CMAPEFA in gaining popular cooperation. Schools taught their students how to recognize FMD and the procedures being used for combating the malady. In addition, the Secretary of Public Education dispatched "cultural brigades" to isolated areas to carry information to the *campesinos*. In April, 1947, the Archbishop of Mexico ordered his clergy to cooperate and tell the faithful of the "sacrifice necessary to limit the diffusion of the pestilence to other regions [of the Republic] and . . . to exterminate it radically." Ecclesiastics in Querétaro distributed a pastoral letter that asked for full cooperation.[34] Priests harangued from the pulpits, often referring to FMD as the *castigo de Dios* (God's punishment) visited upon a sinful nation by a righteous and angry God. Only cooperation could lift the penance from the shoulders of Mexico.[35]

Though by 1950 mass media, field personnel, government agencies, and interested private groups had helped reduce opposition, avarice and corruption had become integral factors in the undercurrent that slowed the campaign. The *mordida* (bribe) was used regularly by cattlemen hoping to ship their cattle out of the infected zone, or for not killing livestock. Corrupt military officials and a few civilian appraisers of livestock, though a minority, lined their pockets with CMAPEFA funds by giving low evaluations, which contributed to reluctance on the part of the peasants to bring in their animals. In Jalisco, *Excelsior* commented that brigades were "committing real sacks . . ." of local pocketbooks.[36]

Co-Director Maurice Shahan nonetheless praised Mexican administrative honesty generally in August, 1947.[37] An exception was General Félix Ireta Viveros, Senator from Michoacán, who became involved in a scandal known as the *danza de los cerdos* (dance of the pigs). Thousands of slaughtered pigs were supposedly buried in fossas in Zinepécuaro and Morelia, but when the fossas were uncovered, only a few hundred pigs were found. This led Oscar Flores to initiate legal proceedings against Ireta, who was accused of participating in a scheme to claim compensation for pigs that had not been slaughtered. The Procurer General dispatched a "special agent . . .

to confront the situation and the powerful men who would pretend to blotch Mexico's prestige. . . ." With formal charges pending, Ireta asked the Senate to excuse him for two months in order to prepare a defense. Former President Lázaro Cárdenas, quoted in *La Prensa,* asked for vigorous punishment for all guilty parties without "distinctions as to class or position," and Ireta retorted that *PRI* officials merely wanted to use him as a scapegoat and to smear him politically. The Mexican Senate, however, asked for maximum penalties for the guilty parties.[38]

Ireta and his accomplices were soon known to the Procurer General, and an official indictment charged them with attempting to defraud the government of 244,320 pesos. Ireta was then arraigned before the Grand Jury of the Chamber of Deputies and was condemned by that body, which declared that "this is the opportunity to prove that Mexico's public life is morally directed." A warrant was issued for Ireta's arrest, he was ousted from the Senate, and he voluntarily presented himself at the Public Ministry in Morelia. Though he faced damning evidence, he continued to protest his innocence; on October 24, 1947, however, he confessed to the falsification of documents. The *PRI* praised Ireta's expulsion from the Senate, and *La Prensa,* a leftist Mexico City tabloid, pointed to Ireta as an example of the unwholesome individuals dominating Mexican political life. It stated that Ireta was "a typical example of the political medium [of Mexico]" based on audacity, frauds, and *compadrazgo.*[39]

Thus, serious opposition was overcome gradually, and in the process, many aides from the United States became cognizant of deep differences between their own culture and that south of the Río Grande. Mexican politics, based on *caudillismo, caciquismo,* and subjective personal relationships, often perplexed and outraged United States officials. Field workers, however, made adjustments and learned to work within the culture of Mexico.

By 1950, direct costs to the United States alone had reached $120 million for the eradication of FMD. The money and that to be added, however, not only eradicated disease but enabled researchers to develop a small body of knowledge about the nature of the malady and contributed significantly to a potential method, vaccination plus limited slaughter entailed in the revised campaign, for control and eradication.[40] Of necessity, the United States sagaciously entered into a cooperative effort that protected its own interests and those of Mexico. It should be noted, however, that some of the conflict over the Brazilian bulls might have been avoided had the State Department upheld consistently the letter of the 1928 treaty with Mexico. A policy decision, however, was made, and aftosa became a threat once again to the United States.

The campaign contributed to Mexican modernization, for mules and tractors began to replace oxen in central Mexico. The malady disposed of some inferior cattle, which were replaced by better stock, and quality was improved by the artificial insemination station at Palo Alto. Successful Mexican-United States cooperation also underscored how far each country had come in its relations with its neighbor, for initial suspicion eventually led to general trust.

Finally, the cooperative effort marked the first and only total commitment on the part of two hemispheric neighbors to eradicate a vicious threat to their economies and standards of living. Political differences notwithstanding, both countries actively undertook to help each other at a time of crisis, and the cooperation served as a model for the entire hemisphere.

CHAPTER V

LATIN AMERICA AND
THE POSTWAR PERIOD

Western South America

Mexico was initiated into the problems of aftosa with a sudden seriousness rarely found in the rest of Latin America, but with the cooperation of the United States, the effects of FMD were mitigated. However, the United States and other countries of the hemisphere afflicted with FMD failed to capitalize on Mexican-United States experience in control and eradication of the malady. Instead, the United States paid little attention to the rest of Latin America during the postwar period and during the cold war. At the same time, the demands of Latin Americans for improved standards of living increased. The shortage of animal protein became increasingly acute in many areas, contributing, in part, to discontent. This unrest caused many Latin American countries to turn to radical governmental alternatives that promised, but failed to deliver, an amelioration of social ills.

Peru, though afflicted sporadically with aftosa since 1910, failed to feel the serious effects of the malady until 1945. Dr. Aurelio Málaga Alba, a veterinarian of the Peruvian government, stated in the *Boletín del Instituto Nacional Anti-Aftosa* that since the end of the war the public health menace imposed by FMD as a result of a decreased amount of animal protein contributed significantly to Peruvian social problems. Peru, according to Málaga, had a sufficient supply of meat and dairy animals. Yet, since FMD had increased in virulence and frequency, Peru was forced into importing meat and milk for the retail market. The result has been increased prices coupled with an intermittent inflationary trend that has plagued Peru since the end of World War II.[1]

While Peru attempted to cope with its FMD problem, Ecuador found that it too had been invaded by aftosa, probably from Colombia, and in July, 1951, the Ecuadoran government initiated the *Campaña para la Prevención de la Fiebre Aftosa* (Campaign to Prevent Aftosa). Prohibitive measures against imports from Colombia were imposed, and stringent border patrol and disinfection programs began. In December, interest groups in Ecuador urged that the efforts of the anti-aftosa campaign continue. Notice was made of Ecuador's obligation not only to eradicate the disease within its own boundaries, but also to recognize the international obligations incumbent upon every country of the hemisphere to prevent the malady. The campaign, however, did not persist.[2]

When it became apparent that aftosa would not simply eradicate itself, the Ecuadoran government again adopted measures to rid the country of the virus in 1956. The interior provinces of Carchi, Imbabura, and part of Pichincha received sanitary brigades from the Centro de Salud Pecuaria (Center of Agricultural Health). In addition, the coastal provinces of Guayas and El Oro were already stricken with the malady along the Pacific.[3] Officials of the Division of Animal Husbandry noted that the disease "has had alarming characteristics regarding the number of affected animals. . . . Losses since January [1956] have been estimated at S/ 10,000,000," with 30 per cent of the livestock affected. The national economy, they stated, was in grave danger, and drastic measures, including slaughter and stringent quarantine, were considered necessary for successful eradication.[4]

The sanitary measures undertaken, however, were not sufficient to eradicate the malady, and additional outbreaks occurred in 1959. Ecuadoran sanitary authorities were informed, and the Pan American Foot-and-Mouth Disease Center dispatched technicians to Ecuador. After studying the situation, Center advisors again urged that drastic measures be used for eradication. Simultaneously with the renewed outbreaks, an international anti-aftosa conference convened in Bogotá with representatives from Colombia, Venezuela, Ecuador, and Panama. The result of the conference was a series of recommendations for eradication of the disease in Ecuador and a strong request that the government take positive action. The Ecuadoran government, in response, created the National Council for Agricultural Defense in October, 1959, composed of representatives of cattlemen's associations, development banks, chambers of agriculture, and the Ministry of Development. In addition, the Pan American Foot-and-Mouth Disease Center sent advisors to the council.

In the following month, the wheels of government were put into motion to obtain funds for the anti-aftosa campaign. The Junta Nacional de Planificación (National Planning Group), the Treasury Ministry, and the United States Embassy worked in concert to obtain funds for Ecuador. By July, 1960, little substantive action had been taken, the administrative machinery moved slowly, and Ecuador failed to provide money to combat aftosa. Also, in 1960, increased outbreaks attested the inability of the Ecuadoran government to cope with the problem, and Dr. Armando Múñoz Noroña wrote to the Division of Animal Husbandry that unless appropriate measures were taken, the result could be catastrophic for Ecuador. Moreover, he noted with alarm the indifference of the government in view of the grave problem.[5]

Ecuador's northern neighbor, Colombia, had been free of FMD until 1951. In 1950, Colombia ordered that all aircraft from FMD countries be disinfected before landing at Colombian airports, but this measure proved of no avail. Venezuelan livestock, infected in 1951, spread the infection to Colombia in the fall of 1951. Slaughter and quarantine operations were promulgated, and the United Nations Food and Agricultural Organization (FAO) dispatched a representative to Panama to establish controls against the spread of the disease from Colombia. In November, the Ministry of Agriculture authorized the purchase of three light Havilland planes and one DC-3 for use in the campaign against FMD. In response to criticism from the FAO representative in Panama, a Colombian veterinarian accused the FAO of vacillation and responsibility for the rapid spread of the disease.[6]

Colombian efforts, however, also took the form of publicizing the differences between aftosa and other vesicular diseases through an official bulletin aimed at cattle raisers.[7] In 1952, losses in milk and livestock were assessed at 9,000 bottles of milk valued at $1,800, and 178 head of cattle with a value of $42,250. In the following year, only six outbreaks were reported in Colombia,[8] but the market in the United States was lost. By 1960, however, canneries and slaughterhouses were established that met United States standards, and canned and fully cured meats were exported to the United States.[9]

Venezuela

Venezuela too began the postwar period facing a serious meat shortage. The Venezuelan government sought to purchase meats from countries whose business it was to export livestock and livestock products. However, regions that were free of aftosa in 1946 included only Ecuador, Colombia, Central America, Mexico, and Venezuela. United States cattle were considered prohibitively expensive, and cattle from FMD-free Latin American countries were insufficient for the demand in Venezuela.[10]

Director of Husbandry, Dr. Claudio Muskus, in a lecture delivered to the Venezuelan-British Cultural Institute entitled "Solutions to the Country's Livestock Problem," noted that other forms of protein must be utilized. He also advocated a reduction of exports, and "the importation of meat, always coming from countries free of diseases unknown in Venezuela, like foot-and-mouth disease, that is economically feasible." Muskus noted the existence of a grave animal production problem in Venezuela. Only 2,800,000 head of cattle existed with as little as a 10 per cent calf crop. Per capita meat consumption, therefore, amounted to only twelve kilograms annually, about one-fourth of the minimum requirement of animal protein. He attributed the shortage to six factors: 1) limited amount of livestock, 2) high calf mortality, 3) poor breeding practices, 4) indiscriminate slaughter of cows, 5) poor range conditions, and 6) livestock diseases such as brucellosis, bovine tuberculosis, and mastitis. Therefore, it became incumbent on the Venezuelan government, warned Muskus, to improve livestock conditions while at the same time taking pains to avoid the introduction of exotic livestock diseases.[11]

When Mexico, one potential source of meat for Venezuela, experienced aftosa outbreaks late in 1946, an order for 10,000 head of Mexican stock was cancelled. Animals recently acquired from Mexico were quarantined at the Venezuelan Quarantine Station on the Isla de la Orchila for ten months, and two high-ranking British veterinarians assisted the Venezuelan government in testing the animals. Nonetheless, efforts to keep meat from FMD countries out of Venezuela failed as the meat deficit became more acute. Violations of Venezuelan statutes became apparent when 148,123 kilograms of Argentine meat were brought into Venezuela in 1947, even though the importation prompted the Ministry of Agriculture to distribute a folder describing FMD to stockmen. More important for the stability of President Rómulo Betancourt's *Junta Revolucionaria,* however, were the resignations of Muskus as Director of Husbandry and Eduardo Mendoza Goiticóa as Minister of Agriculture. Both warned of the risk of importing meat from Argentina, but Ministry of Agriculture efforts to alert consuls and customs officials to the danger went unheeded, because Argentine meat continued to arrive at La Guaira airport.[12]

President Betancourt, in reply to Mendoza Goiticóa, noted that the Junta saw two solutions to the meat shortage: 1) to limit slaughter and begin extensive meat rationing; or 2) to import frozen meat or stock on the hoof. He also pointed out that transport of stock from Colombia was difficult and United States meat was too high in price. Buying high-priced meat meant that only the economically secure citizens of Venezuela could afford a proper amount of meat consumption. Betancourt justified the purchase of Argentine meat because, according to his information, boneless and frozen meat was, theoretically, free of FMD virus. Moreover, a British team of FMD scientists informed the Venezuelan government that the risk would be minimized if the imported meat were consumed in the noncattle raising area, which also eliminated the necessity of slaughtering cows. Farmers could then sell cows to the Banco Agrícola y Pecuaria (Agricultural Bank). With these cows, the Banco, carrying out a policy of redistribution of agricultural wealth, could distribute the cattle to farmers in need of breeding cows. Finally, Betancourt asserted, Argentine meat was certified clean.[13]

In reaction, the Veterinary Society of Venezuela stated that it was obvious the government had failed to understand the veterinarians of the country, since it had accepted the resignations of Muskus and Mendoza Goiticóa. Moreover, Betancourt's statement about boned and frozen meat failed to conform to criteria established by the Society for the protection of the domestic livestock industry. Finally, Dr. Diego Heredia, speaking for the Veterinary Society, warned the government that unless a veterinary commission were established to carry out sanitary functions—including quarantines, embargoes, and training of personnel at home and abroad—the Society washed its hands of any consequences that might befall the country as a result of importations from FMD countries.[14]

Even before aftosa appeared in Venezuela, it had become a political *cause célèbre* when the *Junta Revolucionaria de Gobierno* insisted on the importation of Argentine meats. Pressures from Venezuelan veterinarians, however, led the Junta to decide that greater responsibility for solving technical problems must be given to the Ministry of Agriculture. Thus, *fiebre aftosa* became a permanent preoccupation of the government.[15]

Government concern, however, did not halt the relentless spread of FMD, and in February, 1950, the Regional Veterinary Association of Cojedes informed the Division of Animal Husbandry of the outbreak of a vesicular disease that had occurred in that region and threatened neighboring states. Epithelial samples sent to Pirbright Laboratories in England identified the virus as Type "O" FMD, an analysis already rendered by professors at the Central University of Caracas. Confusion, a not uncommon reaction to an initial FMD outbreak, had led to erroneous diagnoses of vesicular stomatitis, and in a very short time the states of Lara, Yaracuy, Aragua, and Carabobo were affected. Shortly thereafter, a total of sixteen states were included in the affected zone. The Department of Animal Husbandry quickly implemented procedures for obligatory disinfection of cargo vehicles, private cars, busses, and shoes. Within six months, fine cattle haciendas in Venezuela were "turned into hospitals." High-grade bulls and cows died or were slaughtered.[16]

The Junta Militar decreed the creation of Comité Ejecutivo de Lucha contra la Fiebre Aftosa (Executive Committee for the Fight against Aftosa) on July 24 and charged it with the planning of the fight against the malady. An autonomous entity, the Instituto de la Fiebre Aftosa (Aftosa Institute), came into being in August to execute plans, with all resources and facilities to be placed at its disposal.[17]

The Venezuelan government began a vigorous, although sometimes confusing, campaign to combat the disease. Hemispheric and European experts received invitations to advise Venezuela in its efforts to eradicate aftosa. Among the first counselors to arrive was Oscar Flores of Mexico, Co-Director of CMAPEFA. Following the Flores visit, which laid the groundwork for consultative services from Mexico, eighteen Mexican scientists arrived in Venezuela to act as technical advisors. Britain sent Dr. Ian Galloway, Director of Research at Pirbright, who informed Dr. Arnoldo Gabaldón, Director of the Instituto de la Fiebre Aftosa, that an "uncertain, tense, and vacillating" atmosphere existed. Explanations, often contradictory, about aftosa were spread throughout the country, adding even more to the uneasiness. Moreover, nine months were allowed to elapse between the outbreak of the disease and Galloway's recommendation of quarantine and rapid slaughter.[18]

Thus, in an atmosphere of uncertainty, vacillation, and tension, a plan, of sorts, was devised: 1) quarantine, disinfection, and, if necessary, slaughter; 2) intensive vaccination of susceptible animals; and 3) production of an efficient vaccine in sufficient quantities. Initially, Venezuela was forced to use foreign vaccines and, between August, 1950, and February, 1951, 800,000 doses of vaccine were obtained from Amsterdam, Holland. This did not, however, deter Venezuelan veterinarians from a desire to prepare their own vaccine. Under the direction of Dr. Ángel Graciano Castillo, a Laboratory for the Production of Vaccine and Foot-and-Mouth Disease Research was established at Maracay. With its inauguration, vaccine production became a domestic function.[19]

Venezuela, like Mexico, was divided into four zones: 1) a vaccination zone, including the states of Aragua, Apure, Barinas, Carabobo, Cojedes, Falcón, Trujillo, Mérida, Miranda, Yaracuy, Portuguesa, and Zulia; 2) an observation zone, or the District of Cedeño of the state of Bolívar; 3) a freed zone, comprising the states of Monagas and Anzoátequi; and 4) a free zone, the remainder of the country. At the same time the campaign zones were delineated, vaccine production and training of technicians began with the aid of foreign specialists. According to Dr. Carlos Ruíz Martínez, without the informed and practical assistance of many foreign specialists, the control of FMD in Venezuela would have taken much longer.[20]

Much of the energy expended in Venezuela seemed frantic, but it proved advantageous, for the first doses of domestic vaccine were produced in January, 1951, in conjunction with the construction of laboratory and testing facilities. By the end of March, however, a slight setback appeared. Type "A" virus made an appearance around Puerto Cabello and spread as far as Alpargatón and Urama and the fringe of the Carabobo region. The existence of approximately 10,000 animals in the area necessitated the rapid production of 22,000 doses of Type "A" vaccine, which were ready by July.[21]

Two years' effort were required before active cooperation from Venezuelan cattlemen was forthcoming. In May, 1952, members of the Sociedad Regional de Ganaderos de Occidente (Regional Cattlemen's Society of Occidente Province) and other cattlemen proclaimed their satisfaction with the anti-aftosa campaign.[22] At the same time, the vaccine production laboratory worked at a dizzying pace and achieved nearly Herculean results, especially in view of the limited financial and administrative resources given it by the government. In a governmental decree the campaign against FMD was declared to be in the public interest for all of the national territory.[23]

After its initial impulse, FMD lost its aggressiveness in Venezuela, and it was somewhat controlled, though not eradicated. The Instituto de la Fiebre Aftosa fulfilled its function and on June 6, 1953, its autonomy was taken away by governmental decree and passed on to the Department of Husbandry of the Ministry of Agriculture. Research on FMD continued, however, at the Maracay center under the direct authority of the Ministry of Agriculture.[24]

Ruíz Martínez contends that the efforts of the Venezuelan government, its veterinarians, and its cattlemen in the fight against FMD are difficult to appreciate, adding, "Had it not been for foot-and-mouth disease, our country would not be actually suffering the enormous deficit of milk and meat that it is suffering." He further points out that this

grave economic aspect of the problem is not exclusive to Venezuela. It is manifested with the same intensity in all countries that are affected with aftosa. Furthermore, it constitutes a permanent international concern, especially at a time when the world finds itself declaring a massive emergency before hunger and misery from which 500 million human beings are suffering.[25]

Brazil

In Brazil, cattle production in the period immediately after World War II boomed, especially in the state of Minas Gerais. In 1950, twelve million head of cattle roamed the range. Half of these were Zebu stock, and four million were dairy cattle. However, aftosa seemed to be a problem mainly for cattle, not hogs and sheep, and Brazil became increasingly attentive to its FMD problem. Even though it successfully sent stock to Mexico, Brazil nonetheless exerted efforts to at least control the malady that plagued one of its major agricultural industries. Two leading United States veterinarians, who visited Brazil in 1951, reported that of all of the countries they visited—Uruguay, Argentina, Brazil, Chile and Peru—Porto Alegre, Rio Grande do Sul, Brazil, had, at the writing of their report, the best facilities for FMD research.[26]

Despite a marked increase in attention to the problems of FMD, the governments of Getúlio Vargas and his successors failed to conquer the problem by 1957. The *gaúcho* region of Rio Grande do Sul (the interior plains) was infected by all three principal virus types (O, A, and C) by 1957. Infection, however, was notably reduced and the afflicted areas grew smaller. One Brazilian veterinarian stated that as of January, 1957, the reduced incidence of FMD was attributable to two factors: 1) natural immunities resulting from exposure or infection, and 2) large number of vaccinated stock. But he warned that a critical danger existed because of the eventual termination of natural immunities. Vaccine production in Rio Grande do Sul alone totalled nearly 2,740,000 doses, the vast majority being bivalent vaccine. Trivalent vaccine was prepared specifically for stock traveling to cattle shows. In addition to the Instituto de Pesquisas Veterinárias (Institute of Veterinary Research), four private pharmaceutical laboratories produced vaccine, and in 1956 vaccination reached three million head of cattle.[27]

By 1960, however, FMD continued to plague Brazil. She and other members of the South American community suffered not only from political and economic instability engendered by war and postwar adjustments but also from a basic lack of livestock production for export and domestic markets.

Argentina

While Brazil attempted to overcome seemingly insurmountable obstacles in her battle against aftosa, Argentina's anti-Yankee leader, Juan Domingo Perón, also grew increasingly concerned over his country's inability to find sufficient markets for its cattle. In desperation, Perón began making overtures to the United States in an attempt to export livestock and livestock products to that country. Senator Dennis Chávez of New Mexico and other members of Congress, on a trip through South America, were assured by Perón that aftosa no longer posed grave problems for Argentine meat production and export. Miguel Mirando, head of the Argentine National Economic Council, added that Argentina was ready to ship all the beef the United States wanted. It was also noted that in the first six months of 1948, the United States had purchased $12 million worth of canned beef from Argentina as opposed to $300,000 in all of 1947. A final proposal advanced by Perón and Mirando suggested the purchase of fresh Argentine meat by the United States for its occupation forces overseas.[28]

Two years after Senator Chávez and his colleagues visited the Platine Republic, Argentina, Uruguay, and, to some extent, Paraguay, joined at the Fourth Inter-American Conference on Agriculture in efforts to break down United States trade barriers and to obtain higher prices from Great Britain. In addition, the three Platine nations led the fight for a zonal interpretation of existing United States restrictions. All Latin American countries at the meeting accepted the zone theory, but the United States' representatives voiced vigorous dissent.[29]

Argentina failed to penetrate the United States market, and by

1951, foot-and-mouth disease continued to ravage the livestock economy of the area. Buenos Aires, the principal port of Argentina, also served as the primary center for slaughtering activity. Most of the cattle from Córdoba, Santa Fé, Buenos Aires Province, and, to some extent, the littoral provinces of Corrientes and Entre Ríos passed through the many stockyards in Buenos Aires. FMD, however, drastically hindered the domestic trade in livestock because of governmental inability and cattle raisers' reluctance to cooperate in measures to eradicate the malady. All three virus types existed, making effective vaccination of susceptible stock difficult. Perón's government decreed, however, in a futile attempt at least to control the spread of the disease, that all stock entering Buenos Aires must be checked for aftosa when unloaded. If the malady were found, the entire lot of cattle were to be quarantined and slaughtered. This action did not arrest the spread of the disease, however, and almost every day cases of FMD appeared in the yards.[30]

Argentine politics had as its continual theme the increasing need for markets for livestock and the presence of FMD in varying degrees of virulence. New governments succeeding the deposed dictator Perón after 1955 again coped with FMD. In 1957, it became apparent that trivalent vaccine, which had been sold privately for twenty-five years, was the most important weapon in the initiation of an effective campaign against aftosa. In the same year the Congreso Argentino de Fiebre Aftosa (Argentine Aftosa Congress) was created by decree and composed of members of official agencies, private groups, and Government institutions. Its primary objective was obligatory vaccination of all susceptible stock in Argentina. The Comisión Ejecutiva Nacional del Congreso (National Executive Committee of the Congress) and its coordinator were charged with contacting public and private groups and coordinating the renewed effort in the provinces. Added to this group was the Comisión Permanente de Erradicación de la Fiebre Aftosa.[31]

Scientific discoveries at USDA's Plum Island Animal Disease Laboratory further discouraged Argentines' and other Latins' hopes for entering the United States market on a larger scale. On May 13, 1959, the United States banned the importation of salt-cured and unprocessed corned meat from FMD-infected countries. The economic consequence for Argentine was a loss of approximately $30 million annually from its sale of salt-cured beef to the United States.

The United States based its action on much earlier legislation, including the Smoot-Hawley Tariff Act.[32]

This additional ban on Argentine meat produced a great hue and cry in Argentina. In addition to accusing the United States of discrimination, however, the Argentine government continued to take positive, though generally ineffective, steps to eradicate the disease.[33] Receiving impetus from the United States embargo, Argentina decreed that the new eradication program would be financed by a tax that hopefully would make possible a trimester vaccination of at least 40 per cent of the cattle. Compulsory vaccination, it was hoped, would adequately control the disease in order to allow the eventual use of the sanitary rifle only for sporadic outbreaks.[34]

Citing the Argentine experience in 1959 as an example of the problems faced in South America by sanitary authorities, one British expert noted that difficulties in maintaining meticulous sanitary measures could be attributed to: 1) the large ranches and the distances required for proper herd inspection, 2) inadequate numbers of veterinarians and sanitary personnel, and 3) the lack of cooperation from livestock owners. Argentina, specifically, had 44 million cattle, 45 million sheep, 5 million goats, and 4 million pigs in 1959. But only two thousand veterinarians practiced in Argentina, and at times the terrain they had to cover was vast and not traversable. The only method of control seemed to be vaccination. Yet, a vaccination program in a country with inadequate staffs meant that cowhands would have to administer the vaccine, a situation that was not compatible with stringent sanitary measures. Moreover, with cowhands handling the vaccine, field conditions might be such as to render the vaccine useless. Nonetheless, impracticability of the outright slaughter method meant that Argentina was faced with a long-term vaccination project. England, for years a sufferer from FMD, appreciated a decree in Buenos Aires Province requiring vaccination of animals before they left their farms of origin. The decree would "greatly assist in the shorter term to control the risk associated with [England's] meat supplies." [35]

Continuing infection in the stockyards was indicative of the progress of attempts by the Argentine government to eradicate FMD. Any effective approach to FMD eradication in Argentina, it was noted, required international cooperation. An interdependency, both hemispheric and international, developed as a result of Argentine exports to other countries. In addition, buyers would have to cooperate as much as the vendors in guaranteeing proper handling of meat and meat products.[36] United States cooperation was manifested in early 1960 when that country agreed to loan Argentina $14,300,-000 to help her combat FMD. An effective program, stated the Department of State, would give Argentina an opportunity to increase her exportable meat and livestock production.[37]

Varied efforts by the rural societies, cooperatives, schools of veterinary medicine, private laboratories, and government agencies failed to demonstrate full effectiveness in the fight against aftosa. The result was the closing of markets to stock on the hoof by importing countries other than the United States. The loss caused by such closures surpassed 20 million pesos annually. Therefore, the Argentine government again attempted to centralize anti-FMD activities when in July it created the Comisión Asesora Nacional para la Erradicación de la Fiebre Aftosa (CANEFA) (National Planning Commission for FMD Eradication). The new commission was composed of three members: a representative of the Dirección General de Sanidad Animal of the Secretaría de Agricultura y Ganadería, a representative of the Junta Nacional de Carnes, and a coordinating member. Even before the creation of CANEFA, some pilot campaigns with a research orientation began, and provinces such as Santa Fé and La Pampa initiated their own battles against FMD.[38]

When the Twentieth International Livestock Show opened in Buenos Aires, Secretary of Agriculture Ernesto Malacorto announced the creation of CANEFA on July 31, 1960. Malacorto lamented the $180 million exchange loss suffered by his country as a result of the United States' cancellation of its meat orders. Threats of cancellation of meat purchases came from across the Atlantic when West Germany and Britain gave serious consideration to discontinuing their meat imports from the Río de la Plata. The threat, however, was not carried out. Britain's threatened cancellation alone could have resulted in a $300 million loss. Support for the new campaign came immediately from the still powerful Argentine Rural Society when its president, Juan María Mathet, declared that ranchers upheld the principal of obligatory vaccination. The existence of the disease, stated Mathet, caused many customers to discontinue their purchases, and potential customers refused to buy Argentine livestock and livestock by-products.[39]

More government decrees emanated from Buenos Aires shortly after Secretary of Agriculture Malacorto announced the inception of another attempt to control and eradicate aftosa. Unvaccinated cattle and meat coming from such cattle were prohibited entry to slaughterhouses and local markets. In an attempt to keep Patagonia and Tierra del Fuego free of infection, all susceptible animals, in whatever part of Argentina, that were moved south of Río Negro and Neuquén or the part of Buenos Aires Province encompassed by the Río Colorado to the south were required to have an official certificate of vaccination against FMD.[40]

Argentina, along with Brazil, Chile, Peru, Uruguay, Paraguay, and the countries where aftosa later appeared—Colombia and Venezuela —found that governmental decrees accompanied only by inconsistent, sporadic efforts failed to control or to eradicate the dread livestock malady. Moreover, reluctance to use the drastic but effective slaughter method kept directly exposed animals alive and gave potential targets to the virus. The complexity of the infection, which involves at least three viral types and numerous subtypes, also added to the problems faced by the veterinarians of the different countries. The rest of the afflicted Latin American countries, unfortunately, failed to follow Mexico's example of dedication to eradication *per se* through stringent inspection, disinfection, quarantine, and vaccination, as well as slaughter.

Only Central America, the Caribbean, and the United States remained free from the malady in the years between 1946 and 1954. In 1952 Canadian livestock fell prey to the disease, and Canada lost its markets in the United States until the disease was officially declared to have been eradicated in March, 1953. Cuba resisted the temptation to reinstitute bullfighting on the Pearl of the Antilles because Spain, a major source of fighting bulls, had also experienced FMD. Cuban *aficionados,* supported by Spanish promoters, then looked to Mexico and Venezuela for bulls in 1953. Yet, neither country was free of FMD, and the project failed for lack of an acceptable source of fighting bulls.[41]

The Pan American FMD Center

More years of skirmishing with foot-and-mouth disease elapsed before substantive action was taken in the Western Hemisphere to formalize repeated calls for regional cooperation in the control of livestock diseases. The outbreak of FMD in Colombia prompted action on the part of Central American countries and Panama in an attempt to keep their region free of aftosa. Thus, on August 21, 1951, a thirteen-nation conference met in Panama and called for a program of international cooperation to prevent FMD. Their resolutions included a complete exchange of information among the participants, uniform import laws regarding disease carriers and dangerous products, and training expert personnel in all phases of disease control and eradication. The seed for the Organismo Internacional Regional de Salud Agropecuaria (ORISA) was planted; it would serve as a regional organization dedicated to the protection of the livestock economies of the member countries.[42]

Meanwhile, the Organization of American States (OAS) recognized the absolute necessity of coordinating national campaigns in the eradication of foot-and-mouth disease. The Pan American Sanitary Bureau, acting as the executive body for the OAS, formed the Pan American Foot-and-Mouth Disease Center in São Bento, Brazil, under the leadership of Dr. William Henderson. In December, 1951, all OAS members agreed to participate in the maintenance and staffing of the Center. In view of the facilities already available in Brazil, São Bento, five miles north of Rio de Janeiro, was selected as the site. An area of 227 acres was provided by the Brazilian government, including the structures already on the property. Brazil also undertook the construction of additional units, laboratories, and stables, and the initial cost to Brazil was 10 million cruzeiros or $530,000. Once in operation, the Center's first annual budget was $210,000. In addition, a special appropriation of $165,341 from the United States in 1951 helped launch the Center. Even Brazil, with its inflationary problems, its expensive government, and its cost incurred in constructing the Center, additionally contributed 251,632 cruzeiros.[43]

Once operative, the Center had two principal objectives: 1) to maintain free from aftosa those areas not yet contaminated, and 2) "to assist the affected countries to control and eventually eradicate the disease." In addition, special diagnostic services and basic research complemented the Center's objectives. To attain these ends, those who established the Center conceived its four functions to be: 1) training, 2) laboratory diagnosis, 3) consultative field services, and 4) research.[44] In 1952, for example, 104 specimens were received for diagnosis at the Center, and the results were dispatched immediately to the affected countries. In addition, at the Panama meeting of 1951, FAO agreed with Panama that two technicians to coordinate preventive programs in Central America and the Caribbean were necessary for successful consummation of the objectives of the meeting. The FMD Center trained both technicians before they arrived in Panama.[45]

Within three years of its creation, the FMD Center answered requests for assistance from Venezuela, Costa Rica, and British Guiana. At the request of the Venezuelan government, it performed an evaluation of that nation's national anti-FMD program. Costa Rica, a country in the free zone, called upon Center technicians to help establish preventive facilities. The rapid spread of FMD in northern Brazil prompted British Guiana to call for assistance in the establishment of adequate patrol methods to protect its area. In addition, Center staff members developed educational materials for use by the different countries of the hemisphere. A film, *Brote,* and a booklet, *El Magnífico Toro,* were produced in 1954 as media for educating the cattle raisers of Latin America to the dangers and implications of FMD. Both items, it was reported, were in heavy demand.[46]

As part of its training program, the Center sponsored regional training courses. A course in preventive measures was prepared for North America (United States and Mexico), Central America, and the Caribbean. For northern South America (Venezuela, Colombia, Ecuador, Peru, and Bolivia), the Center began a course in prevention, control, and eradication of FMD. Finally a third course for countries where aftosa occurred frequently—Brazil, Chile, and the countries of the Río de la Plata—emphasized intensive control programs preparatory for ultimate eradication of the disease.[47]

As part of its function, the Center acted as liaison with other regional and international agencies dedicated to the eradication of FMD, such as OIRSA. In addition, the Center sponsored two seminars in 1955, one in Bogotá in June and the other in Rio de Janeiro in November. Of particular significance, the Bogotá meeting viewed aftosa as a serious hemispheric problem conquerable only through regional cooperation.[48]

When World War II ended, the United States directed its primary attentions to reconstructing Europe and democratizing Japan. Little if any attention was paid to Latin America's critical problems that were partly the result of wartime economic and social dislocations and postwar adjustments. Serious economic and social problems, including aftosa, deeply rutted the already eroded soil of inter-American relations. In only one instance—United States cooperation with Mexico—did active participation through more than counsel and monetary aid from the United States help ameliorate a serious health problem. After 1950, however, the rapid spread of aftosa made all members of the OAS increasingly aware of its real dangers. Regional agencies inside and outside the OAS attempted to work in concert to resolve a serious livestock problem. Yet, the work of these agencies met constant setbacks as a result of political and economic instability throughout most of South America. Programs were begun but not continued, as in Argentina, and the disease, refusing to recognize rest periods, spread especially during times of inactivity in control and eradication measures.

CHAPTER VI

AFTOSA IN THE SIXTIES I

When John F. Kennedy was elected President of the United States he maintained that Latin America was one of the most critical areas of the world. Its population growth was mushrooming and outstripping existing food supplies. After his inauguration Kennedy proclaimed an Alliance for Progress, a self-help program designed to enable the Latin Americans, with United States assistance, to strengthen their societies and economies by bringing about more equitable distribution of wealth. In part, Kennedy's motive was purely political: the success of Fidel Castro in Cuba posed a threat to the United States and other countries of the hemisphere, and Kennedy hoped to woo the republics south of the Rio Grande from the influences of Communism. Little, if any, emphasis was put upon increasing agricultural output to meet the needs of the burgeoning population and to help stabilize the wavering economies of some countries. Land and tax reforms were conceptualized as twin panaceas for Latin America's multiple problems. Yet, the disruptive effects of land and tax reforms tended to create even further imbalances in Latin American exports and in the economic, political, and social structures of the more backward republics. Campaigns against FMD followed the same course as those of the 1950's. Programs were begun, but sometimes because of radical changes in political regimes, they were discontinued or they suffered from general inattention.

Argentina

Argentina, still one of the major meat exporters in Latin America, persisted in her efforts to sell meat from Tierra del Fuego to the United States, and in late 1960 Argentine Minister of Commerce Carlos Juni again requested that meat from the free area of the republic be allowed to enter the United States. As before, the request was denied by the USDA.[1] Refusal on the part of the United States prompted Argentina to try again in its efforts to eradicate aftosa, and on January 1, 1961, the Minister of Agriculture decreed that in all places where a heavy concentration of cattle existed disinfection baths and vehicle disinfection stations were to be built. Another decree affirmed that all infected cattle south of the Ríos Lista, Chico, and Santa Cruz were to be slaughtered, following the precedent established by the provinces of Santa Fé and La Pampa.[2]

The vaccination program undertaken by Argentina aimed primarily at maintaining a buffer zone around Patagonia, Tierra del Fuego, and La Pampa. In addition, over 80 per cent of the livestock in Buenos Aires Province, one of the principal export livestock production centers in Argentina, were to receive vaccinations. Motivation for this action was twofold: The United Kingdom and West Germany were seriously considering a curtailment of imports of Argentine meat; and the United States, seeing the efforts of Argentina to maintain Tierra del Fuego free from disease through the creation of a buffer zone, might relent and allow the entrance of mutton from that area.[3]

At the Punta del Este Conference in August, 1961, the charter that stated the principles of the Alliance for Progress was formally subscribed to by all hemispheric participants. Despite the frustrated attempt in April, 1961, to forcibly oust Castro from Cuba, President Kennedy's efforts to make himself popular in Latin America showed a marked contrast to the indifference of the Truman and Eisenhower years. His youthful good looks, a Spanish-speaking wife, lovely children, and Catholic religion made Kennedy appealing to a majority of Latin Americans; and his obvious concern for the problems of his hemispheric neighbors pointed, at least initially, to an improvement in inter-American relations.

Thus, in an atmosphere of good will and a supposedly renascent Good Neighbor Policy, Arturo Frondizi, President of Argentina, met with Kennedy after the Punta del Este meeting and requested that the United States reevaluate its position on meat importations from Tierra del Fuego.[4] True to his promise to reconsider the Argentine meat problem, Kennedy formed a panel of experts under the President's Science Advisory Committee to consider the scope of the aftosa problem and its possible solutions. In turn, the panel asked a group of food technologists, veterinarians, and other scientists to meet in December to study the feasibility of a multidisciplinary approach to FMD control and eradication and the subsequent implications for the food industry.[5]

The interdisciplinary panel recommended that a mission be sent to Argentina, and Kennedy, in line with Frondizi's request, dispatched a group under the chairmanship of Dr. J. George Harrar, who was soon to become President of the Rockefeller Foundation. Argentine counterparts headed by Dr. Bernardo Houssay, endocrinologist and Nobel Laureate, worked side by side with the Harrar group. They discussed problems brought on by the recent United States embargo on salt-cured beef. According to the *Journal of the American Veterinary Medical Association,* "The loss of the market by the Argentines and packers in South American countries also concerned the United States because of its desire to strengthen the general economy and increase its resistance to communistic influences." The interdisciplinary panel's mission, it continued, was to "assess the current situation on foot-and-mouth disease and determine whether the application of science and technology" would free meat of viable virus and thereby allow its importation into the United States.[6]

Within two months after the Harrar mission's visit to Argentina, United States and Argentine delegates held a formal conference in Washington, D.C. Representatives from the Pan American Health Organization and from the United States National Academy of Science-National Research Council, and members of the Executive

Office of the President of the United States and of the Departments of State, Defense, and Agriculture also joined the conferences. During the meeting they outlined an organization for the scientific support and coordination of participation by Argentina, the United States, and the Pan American Health Organization in several programs. Moreover, the conference resulted in the formation of an Argentine-United States Joint Commission on FMD.[7]

United States cattlemen were quick to presume a potential threat in the Joint Commission. The *American Cattle Producer* reopened the fight that occurred in the 1930's over the proposed United States-Argentine Sanitary Convention and noted in 1962 a resurgence of a conciliatory attitude on the part of the United States government. It asserted that cattlemen in the United States opposed the importation of Argentine meat for sanitary reasons and charged that the investigating committee would do nothing but raise false hopes among the Argentines. When the American National Cattleman's Association met in Tampa, Florida, in January, 1962, members expressed the hope in the form of a formal resolution that the mission to Argentina would include regulatory officials and prominent members of the cattle industry. They further resolved that

> in the interest of the welfare of our industry and the consuming public at large, we emphatically urge upon our administration and the Congress that no change be made in our present sanitary laws or regulations that would permit importation of cattle or beef from so-called "free zones" in foot-and-mouth infected countries.[8]

The Harrar mission submitted a preliminary report to the President's Science Advisory Committee in March, 1962. It stated that Argentina's main concerns were the loss of North American and other markets for cured beef and that bulk-cooked meat produced in some *frigoríficos* as required by the USDA limited its commercial acceptability in the United States. Moreover, the question of Tierra del Fuego continued as the counterpart of United States-Argentine agricultural relations. The scientific mission recommended: 1) cured and cooked beef research, 2) sending USDA scientific personnel to Argentina, 3) a joint survey of Tierra del Fuego, and 4) strengthening the Pan American Foot-and-Mouth Disease Center in Brazil. Argentine officials maintained that the major issues involved problems related to cured and cooked beef and felt that these two points were of "over-riding importance for political and psychological, as well as economic reasons." [9]

Again, the *American Cattle Producer* dissented from the United States government's position of exploring at least the possibility of importations from Tierra del Fuego. It noted that by sending United States scientists and technicians to Argentina a dangerous precedent was established because the USDA was forced to prove the dangers of FMD. They added, moreover, that "some of the scientists . . . said that political expediency could override scientific findings. If this should happen, if the scientists' warnings . . . should become sub-servient to political maneuvers, then the cattle industry would be in real trouble." Cattlemen in the United States feared that the combina-tion of Argentine interest in exporting to the United States and Ken-nedy's desire "to improve relations with the Latin American nations" seriously threatened the United States cattle industry.[10]

Cattlemen's protests, however, were overridden, and the Joint United States-Argentine Commission met in formal session in No-vember, 1962. Argentina, along with other South American coun-tries, maintained that the United States could import their beef without high risk if certain discriminatory requirements were lifted and if strict quarantine methods were followed. The Joint Commis-sion, however, felt that such a position was premature. Experimenta-tion to ascertain the survival of FMD virus in cured beef from both vaccinated and unvaccinated stock was necessary. An Argentine-United States protocol was drawn up for such a study, and a pro-posal for an epizoötiological survey of Tierra del Fuego was in-cluded.[11]

In an attempt to expand its anti-FMD activities, Argentina enlarged the zone of her national campaign to encompass all of the provinces of Buenos Aires, San Luis, and Entre Ríos and parts of Santa Fé and Córdoba.[12] Along with an expansion of Argentine campaign plans, the United States announced in February, 1963, its cooperative program with the Platine Republic to determine the per-sistence of infective virus in cured beef from vaccinated animals. Funding for the program came from the Agency for International Development (AID).[13]

Political changes, including the overthrow of President Frondizi in

1962, did not deter the Joint Commission from its efforts to carry out its proposed program. The United States continued to permit imports of some animal products from Argentina under strict USDA supervision, such as glands for biological and pharmaceutical uses. The USDA argued that under proper laboratory conditions the risk was extremely low.[14]

Experimentation on the persistence of FMD virus in the lymph nodes of vaccinated and unvaccinated cattle began in 1963 at the Plum Island Animal Disease Laboratory with biological samples supplied cooperatively by CANEFA and USDA representatives in Argentina. The results led the Joint Commission to report that vaccination "markedly reduced the chances of recovering virus from lymph nodes at the time of slaughter of cattle exposed to virus thirty-two hours previously." In addition, tentative conclusions were drawn about meat that had been cured for approximately one month. The Joint Commission noted that the incidence of virus in unvaccinated meat that had been cured for one month was appreciably reduced. They cautioned, however, that insufficient data kept them from making a conclusive statement about the degree of risk of active virus in cured meat.[15]

During the time the joint experiments were underway, Argentina continued to extend the horizons of the anti-FMD campaign, by creating the Servicio de Luchas Sanitarias (Sanitary Campaign Service, or SELSA). In September, four members were designated as consultants for SELSA: two from the Confederaciones Rurales Argentinas; one from the Argentine Rural Society and one from the Confederación Intercooperativa Agropecuaria (Intercooperative Agricultural Production Confederation). SELSA was presided over by the Director General de Sanidad Animal, and was given the following functions: 1) apply proper animal health norms, 2) approve and evaluate sanitary campaigns, 3) coordinate the action of the local commissions, 4) prepare a general budget and help in the preparation of local anti-FMD budgets, 5) secure personnel, 6) administer general funds, and 7) negotiate conventions with national, provincial, and municipal entities in the fight against aftosa. Moreover, a technical corps of administrators and scientists planned and conducted the sanitary programs and controlled the national production of veterinary products. Local commissions headed by SELSA veterinarians carried out nationally prepared plans, and the Consejo Consultivo, made up of representatives of various interest groups, kept the administration of SELSA informed of the politico-economic conditions that evolved in the FMD campaigns.[16]

Thus, while Argentina again attempted to centralize and make more efficient its anti-FMD efforts through the creation of the nearly omnipotent, autonomous SELSA, the second proposal of the Joint Commission—the epizoötiological survey of Tierra del Fuego—was initiated. In July, 1963, at a meeting of representatives from Paraguay, Brazil, Uruguay, Argentina, and Chile, and with collaboration by the Pan American Aftosa Center, an Argentine-Chilean Commission for the Prevention of Foot-and-Mouth Disease was created for a joint survey of Tierra del Fuego, a possession of both countries. Ultimately, both Argentina and Chile declared that all livestock from the mainland were to be vaccinated before crossing to the island, all milk was to undergo pasteurization, and livestock feed was to receive a cleansing treatment. A statement from the United States-Argentine Commission declared:

> For the evaluation of the risk in treating the island [Tierra del Fuego] as an area separate from the mainland country for the purpose of importing fresh meat into the United States, the determination of presence or absence of foot-and-mouth disease is not the only consideration. Other factors, such as trade and commerce between the island and the mainland, must be taken into account.

Such a declaration prompted Chile and Argentina to tighten their sanitary controls regarding Tierra del Fuego.[17]

The Joint Survey of Tierra del Fuego found no evidence of the existence of FMD or other vesicular diseases. The Argentine-Chilean Commission did, however, have something to say about maintaining the area free of disease when they noted:

> . . . special attention must be given to the movement of all livestock, products of animal origin, or of any other products that might be contaminated with foot-and-mouth disease virus. These points have been discussed by the national authorities in Argentina and Chile, separately and together, and also in collaboration with the Pan American Foot-and-Mouth Disease Center.[18]

Meanwhile, *The New York Times* reported that the three-year vaccination program begun in 1960 showed impressive results, for CANEFA reported only 770 infected premises between January and June, 1963. Estimates as to the length of time required for eradication, however, varied from an optimistic guess of seven to ten years to a probably more realistic one of nine to twenty years. All estimates indicated that a good deal of money, probably $1–3 billion, would be necessary for a successful eradication program.[19]

Favorable reports of the successes of the vaccination program prompted a former vice-president of Armour Meats to declare that an additional 100,000 tons of Argentine meat would not make an appreciable difference in United States meat prices. He did point out that despite shipping costs Argentine beef still undersold that of the United States because of the difference in basic production costs. United States Ambassador to Argentina Root McClintock indicated to the Argentine government that with the eradication of FMD, the export value of Platine meat of $12 million per year could be escalated to $50 million without hurting United States domestic prices.[20]

Argentina continued her efforts to keep the southern provinces of the republic free of foot-and-mouth disease. Obligatory vaccination remained as a prerequisite for entry of cattle into the area south of the Río Colorado, and SELSA expanded its activities in the fall of 1963 to include the rest of Córdoba, Santa Fé, and all of Mendoza, San Juan, Corrientes, Misiones, and parts of the Chaco and La Rioja.[21]

In the ensuing year Argentina made no remarkable progress, and by 1965 there was an apparent decline in the intensity of efforts to eradicate the malady that cursed her livestock export industry. By mid-August Argentina reported a total of 4,286 infected premises beginning in the east and northeast of Buenos Aires Province. The disease, apparently one of high virulence, spread through the Pampas and south of Córdoba and central Santa Fé. In response to the new threat, SELSA devised a complex battle plan that demarcated a free zone, a buffer zone, and an infected zone and had as its primary objective the establishment of a sanitary cordon around Tierra del Fuego.[22]

Throughout 1966 Argentina struggled in her attempts at eradication through vaccination and absolutely minimal slaughter operations, and in early 1967, Dr. Carlos Palacios, Director, Pan American Foot-and-Mouth Disease Center, and Ing. Edgardo Seoane, acting in behalf of the Pan American Health Organization, reported that approximately 90 per cent of all Argentine cattle received vaccine injections three times a year. They concluded that Argentina "had the best organized national foot-and-mouth disease campaigns, and that close contacts were maintained with the Center." Despite the seeming efficiency of its organization, Argentina's last hope for entrance into the United States market faded. Early in January, 1967, Argentine officials reluctantly announced that Tierra del Fuego, the only area in Argentina previously known to be free of FMD, was infected with the disease (Type "C"). The virus that penetrated Tierra del Fuego caused 350 deaths among 900 head of cattle on one premise. Good fortune prevailed, however, for the farms in Tierra del Fuego are separated by long distances and the malady apparently was isolated on one farm. The infected farm was quarantined, and the legal measures for slaughter of infected and exposed stock were given consideration. Thus, Argentina, which had endeavored to hold Tierra del Fuego as the final bastion to aftosa, found that even this had crumbled.[23]

Uruguay and Paraguay

Uruguay, too, faced obstacles in controlling FMD and failed to overcome it in the 1960's. Three virus types were enzoötic in the area, and in 1962 Uruguay experienced a series of outbreaks that further debilitated that nation's livestock industry. The Uruguayan government declared that the anti-aftosa battle was obligatory in all the national territory.[24] Five years later, when Palacios and Seoane visited Uruguay, they reported that even though vaccination was not compulsory, approximately 50 per cent of the cattle had received annual vaccinations. In addition, Uruguay hoped to complete vaccine testing laboratories by 1969.[25]

Cognizant of the necessity of eradicating the disease for the benefit of its own economy, Uruguay applied to the Inter-American Development Bank for external credit to finance its campaign. That country indicated that it would conduct studies in preparation for a final application and would provide for a well-defined plan and an autonomous agency to administer the program that would be free from the vicissitudes of political change. A requirement for mass, systematic compulsory vaccination would also be included.[26]

To overcome a basic transportation problem in the battle against FMD, Uruguay entered into an agreement with Brazil under the auspices of the Regional Animal Health Commission (Uruguay, Paraguay, Argentina, Brazil, and Chile). In exchange for heavy vehicles, Uruguay pledged to supply Brazil with high-grade cattle to help the latter improve its herds.[27]

Political change came to Uruguay in early 1967, and Seoane and Palacios were unable to extract written pledges of monetary support for the Pan American Aftosa Center from the Ministers of Health and External Relations. Later in the year, however, the Uruguayan Minister of Agriculture confirmed his country's financial commitment to the Center in a letter to José A. Mora, Secretary General of the OAS.[28]

Paraguayan cattle also showed evidence of FMD and its disastrous consequences in the 1960's. Officials from Paraguay wrote that because of aftosa some of the best markets for export meat were closed to their country. The United States, Central America, Mexico, and Caribbean countries refused to import fresh and frozen meat from disease-afflicted areas. Venezuela and Colombia, which seemingly had achieved minor successes in controlling the malady, refused to purchase breeding stock from Paraguay for fear of introducing yet another virus type into their national territories. Moreover, the countries of the European Common Market, perhaps using FMD as a pretext, severely limited the importation of Paraguayan meats.[29] The Pan American Aftosa Center, in an attempt to encourage Paraguay in its anti-aftosa campaign, calculated that a loss of 25 per cent was a conservative estimate for the damage that FMD had done to Paraguay. Paraguay, it was believed, lost over a billion guaraníes annually.[30]

Paraguay, despite its domestic and international problems, especially in the realm of commerce, recognized the necessity of regional cooperation to eradicate aftosa. Therefore, in February, 1962, Paraguay joined with its neighbors of the southern cone in Montevideo to confer on the problems of enzoötic aftosa. Paraguayan officials stated that "Paraguay is obligated to carry fourth its anti-aftosa campaign nationally and multinationally." [31]

Slow to begin its campaign, Paraguay nonetheless began the formulation of a plan to defeat the malady. Official statements indicated that Paraguay hoped to utilize the experience of other countries in the elaboration of its anti-FMD campaign. While drawing upon the experiences of others, Paraguayan technicians were careful to note that factors of agricultural and cultural idiosyncracies of the peasants and material possibilities of the nation needed consideration. At this writing, the strategy devised by Paraguay has seemed to follow the same general pattern as that of the other countries: establishment of clean, buffer, and infected zones; stringent quarantines; systematic, massive, obligatory vaccination; and the creation of an independent, apolitical agency, the Servicio Nacional de Lucha Contra la Fiebre Aftosa or the National Service for the Fight Against Aftosa (SENALFA). A plan such as that devised by Paraguay, officials were quick to note, cannot succeed without the cooperation of the cattlemen who must be convinced of the necessity of inspection, quarantine, and, if necessary, slaughter. Compensation for slaughtered stock was also a factor under study by the Paraguayan government.[32]

Paraguayan officials felt that the initiation of an anti-aftosa campaign should begin immediately, for it was the last country in the southern cone to take even preliminary measures against the infection. Official statements pointed out that Argentina renewed its efforts in 1961 and that Rio Grande do Sul, Brazil, began massive obligatory vaccinations in December, 1965, in addition to activities already underway in Paraná, Rio de Janeiro, and São Paulo. Uruguay, after the completion of its laboratories in September, 1966, began its national campaign. Paraguay, therefore, felt a responsibility to live up to its international agreements and joined quickly in the battle against the menace.[33]

In early 1966, Paraguay became the first country to prepare its application for aid from the Inter-American Development Bank (IDB) and hoped to be the first nation to benefit from financial assistance from that agency to defeat aftosa. In 1965, the IDB agreed to provide Paraguay with $15,000 for the recruitment of consultants to assist in the establishment of economic and sanitary defense against FMD. The Paraguayan application included a request for a loan of $933,000, or approximately 75 per cent of the estimated cost of an anti-aftosa campaign for a five-year period. The money was designated for construction of a laboratory and the acquisition of equipment and materials. The IDB required ratification of the treaty between itself and Paraguay by legislative action of the country, and in March, 1966, the House of Representatives of Paraguay was reported to be giving careful study to the arrangement.[34]

In the following year, drastic upward revisions were made in the initial plan to be submitted to the IDB. Collaboration on the part of a planning company from Brazil, the FMD Center, and Paraguayan technicians raised the monetary request to 50 per cent of the cost of the campaign over a five-year period, or $3,500,000. Obviously, Paraguay had greatly underestimated the initial cost. When Seoane and Palacios visited Paraguay, however, they discovered that the national plan and the financing were being delayed by "political and budgetary difficulties." [35] In short, difficulty was encountered in the establishment of an administrative and technical agency with sufficient autonomy to administer the anti-aftosa campaign effectively. To promote the establishment of such an agency, Seoane and Palacios conferred with President Alfredo Stroessner, members of the Cabinet, representatives of the Paraguayan Livestock Owner's Association, and the Permanent Parliamentary Commission. They also appealed for help to the newspapers, which responded by publicizing the dangers of FMD to the Paraguayan economy. Efforts by Palacios and Seoane bore fruit because on January 27, 1967, the Minister of Agriculture informed them of a parliamentary offer to approve a law that established an autonomous agency. Moreover, he added, the plan and project were ready, and a preliminary IDB application was being prepared. In drawing up the request for external financial assistance, the Pan-American FMD Center came to the aid of Paraguay.[36]

The plan presented to the IDB included the construction of a laboratory for vaccine production. When the laboratory became operative, it would no longer be necessary to rely upon private pharmaceutical houses in Argentina. Domestic financing was to come through a new tax on cattle sales amounting to 50 *guaraníes* per head; this was expected to net the government approximately 30 to 40 million *guaraníes* annually. As required by the IDB, vaccination was to be compulsory and systematic. One additional policy to the vaccination phase was begun, however: wealthy ranchers were required to pay for the vaccine while peasants would receive it free.[37]

Chile

Chile, like other members of the southern zone of chronically afflicted FMD countries, also faced severe aftosa problems and it also sought to avail itself of international funding through the IDB for its anti-aftosa campaign. Like some of her South American neighbors, Chile did not require compulsory mass vaccination, and the existing production laboratory was not an autonomous agency but a part of the Bacteriological Institute under the Ministry of Health. Chilean officials, however, recognized the burdensome nature of this arrangement and informed Seoane and Palacios that a study was underway to transfer those sections of the Institute that dealt with aftosa and vaccine production to the Ministry of Agriculture.[38]

As early as 1965, the Ministry of Agriculture received a preliminary draft of a plan destined for presentation to the IDB, and an application was formally submitted in 1966. In a budgeted project of $10 million for a six-year period, Chile hoped to raise 80 per cent of the required funds through government initiative and the cooperation of the livestock owners. The remaining 20 per cent was requested from the IDB. However, Chile failed to make a provision in its plan for an autonomous agency for program execution. This obstacle was surmounted when the government granted sufficient autonomy to the Bacteriological Institute for execution of the control and eradication program without being subject to the exigencies of political pressure and patronage.[39]

To complicate further Chile's aftosa problem, the FMD outbreak on the Argentine side of Tierra del Fuego created alarm among Chilean technicians and livestock men when reports reached them that more than a month had elapsed before the disease in Tierra del Fuego was reported by Argentine health authorities. A request was sent to the FMD Center for cooperation in order to assure that an epizoötiological survey would be made to define the extent of the outbreak. Palacios and Seoane proposed a meeting of the Joint Argentine-Chilean Commission to define the measures to be taken as a result of FMD in Tierra del Fuego.[40]

In addition, Chilean specialists submitted three programs to Seoane and Palacios that they believed should be carried out by the FMD Center. First, they suggested that the Center compile, evaluate, and recommend techniques for the administration of national anti-aftosa campaigns. Secondly, they underscored the need for epizoötio-logical studies conducted under the auspices of the Center. Finally, new types of vaccine and vaccination techniques were necessary to advance the battle against FMD. As a general recommendation, the Chileans contended that in view of the national campaigns undertaken by the South American countries periodic meetings be held to exchange ideas and to help resolve common problems. Such meetings, it was suggested, should be included in the plans of the Regional Animal Health Technical Commission of the Southern Cone. When Seoane and Palacios met with President Eduardo Frei Montalvo and the Ministers of External Affairs, Health, and Agriculture they emphasized the necessity of organizing national campaigns that would later be coordinated at the regional level.[41]

When Seoane and Palacios began discussions of the annual assessment asked of Chile for the support of the FMD Center, Chilean officials, despite the many services rendered to Chile by the Center— including agreements on modified live virus vaccine, help in the preparation of the first draft of the IDB application, serological testing of Tierra del Fuego, and the formulation of the Joint Chilean-Argentine Commission—considered Chile's portion too high. The country was assessed only 2.09 per cent of the Center's total budget, or $25,139 annually, to which Chile agreed.[42]

In the period of the 1960's the United States embarked on a concerted campaign to improve its complicated relations with most of the Latin American republics. Its Alliance for Progress promised hope for more equitable distributions of wealth through land and tax reforms. At the same time, comparatively little attention was directed to the food problems that plague present-day Latin America. During the current decade a series of national anti-aftosa campaigns began with varying degrees of success in controlling the malady. South American problems of political and bureaucratic origins have hampered these attempts to rid the continent of one of its greatest animal health problems and thereby increase the domestic and export potential of the livestock industries of the several countries.

CHAPTER VII

AFTOSA IN THE SIXTIES II

Brazil

While Argentina struggled to maintain her anti-FMD program on a substantial level and other South American countries tried to control at least the spread of the malady, Brazil coped with the three major FMD virus types diffused throughout most of the country in 1963.[1] At the same time, the Brazilian government continued to some extent its construction program at the FMD Center in São Bento. The new building program reached a cost of 32 million cruzeiros for 1963.[2]

Two years later Rio Grande do Sul, one of the most important stock producing areas in the country, suffered a highly virulent outbreak that continued unchecked into 1967. Though Brazilian sanitary authorities attempted to control the spread of the malady through the administration of vaccine on a progressive, regional basis, they were impeded by the inability of laboratory and technical resources to produce vaccine in sufficient quantities.[3]

When Seoane and Palacios visited Brazil early in 1967, they learned of Brazilian intentions to apply for a loan from the IDB. The amount of the loan, $21 million, was to supplement a total cost of $70 million for a five-year period. Of the total amount budgeted by Brazil to combat aftosa, $5 million was earmarked for loans to vaccine-producing laboratories. Seoane and Palacios were asked to expedite the loan application.[4] During the period 1965–1967, Brazilian vaccine production rose from 25 million doses to 40 million, partly because of the loan from IDB. Brazil continued to support the Pan-American FMD Center, for the Center proved during the 1960's to be an extremely useful agency for assistance to Brazil. It helped in the preparation of the IDB loan application, aided Brazil in the conduct of experiments with live virus, tested vaccines, and assisted with a pilot vaccination project in Ianhandu.[5]

Venezuela

In Northern South America, Venezuela seemed to have achieved at least a stalemate with the virus. Dr. Carlos Ruíz Martínez, Venezuela's permanent delegate to the International Office of Epizoötics, addressed the twenty-fourth general session of that group in 1961. He informed them that the disease continued but that slow, gradual progress was being made toward its diminution. He pointed out that fewer loci of infection existed and that the infected zone was being reduced. Moreover, he noted, the virus had adapted to the environment and the animals seemed to be less susceptible to the virus. There were, in addition, periods of relative calm when it seemed that FMD was not present in Venezuela.[6] Ruíz Martínez continued that a consistent control effort in Venezuela was the rule. Systematic vaccination of susceptible livestock and control of animal movements from one zone to another were practiced, and disinfection was constantly carried out. He declared that all sanitary procedures were practiced scrupulously.[7]

Enforcement of sanitary regulations notwithstanding, in late 1962 the Venezuelan army impounded 400 head of smuggled Colombian cattle valued at 300,000 bolivares in Puerto Páez. Three well-known cattlemen were arrested by the Guardia Nacional for smuggling. Such activity led Venezuelan authorities to believe that precautions were not taken seriously in the region, and the government estimated that four or five thousand head of Colombian cattle were introduced in this way.[8]

Venezuela, a constant promoter of cooperative measures to eradicate FMD, joined the second Inter-American meeting on Animal Production in Baurú, Minas Gerais, Brazil, under the auspices of the Brazilian Ministry of Agriculture and the University of São Paulo in 1962. In a spirit of interchange of ideas, the Venezuelan delegation shared with the other delegates the means by which it attempted to eliminate the malady from its soil.[9]

By the time Seoane and Palacios met with Venezuelan leaders in early 1967, they were informed that Venezuela did not, in fact, need external financing for its anti-aftosa campaign. The Minister of Agriculture contended that the IDB should put more of its resources into the campaigns conducted by Venezuela's neighbors. By so doing, Venezuela herself would indirectly benefit from the neighboring campaigns because external threats of infection would be eventually eliminated.[10] Taking advantage of the receptive mood in which they found the Venezuelans, Seoane and Palacios emphasized the importance of the Pan-American FMD Center. They also discussed the economic aspects of FMD and noted that FMD presented a huge barrier to trade within the Latin American Free Trade Association (LAFTA). Moreover, echoing Venezuelan sentiment, they underscored the absolute necessity of coordinating national campaigns.[11]

Colombia

Colombia, one of the countries in South America with great potential for livestock production, had experienced a "severe wave of infection" in 1963. By the time Seoane and Palacios reached Colombia in February, 1967, the problem was still far from solution. They considered their Colombian visit of utmost importance because Colombia was embroiled in a dispute over the Chocó region and because Panama, bordering on Colombia, was the southern terminus of the disease-free zone.[12]

Carlos Lleras Restrepo, President of Colombia, felt that the conflict between his country and OIRSA (see page 102 for evolution of OIRSA) needed quick resolution (see below). He declared that because of the latent danger to Central America in stocking the Chocó with livestock, "Colombia will not vacillate in sacrificing her own interests since those of neighboring republics are worth more and should be protected and whose prosperity Colombia does not wish to see affected [adversely] in any manner." So strongly did Lleras Restrepo feel about the problem that he authorized Seoane and Palacios to circulate his statement to the members of OIRSA.[13]

As of 1967, Colombia faced severe problems because only 25 per cent of its cattle received regular vaccinations. The risk was especially high, for a new wave of the epizoötic would create havoc in the herds. It was apparent that the causes for the low vaccination level derived from a lack of concern and knowledge on the part of livestock raisers as well as a paucity of adequate resources for vaccination. With regard to the first point, Seoane and Palacios recommended no loans be given to stock raisers for unvaccinated cattle, a prohibition against cattle movements without the corresponding vaccination certificates, and an intensified educational campaign. Colombian authorities initiated a study to obtain external financing for the campaign. The budget for the campaign would be arranged so that both government and livestock raisers would contribute to the total cost of the program. In addition, since the Colombian Animal Health Institute produced only eight million doses of vaccine annually, it became apparent that an increase in production was necessary in view of the proposed plans.[14]

Northern Colombia, specifically the departments of northern Antioquia, Córdoba, Atlántico, Magdalena, La Goajira, and northern Santander, became the area of concentration for an intensified campaign because the northern provinces encompassed 17,000 square kilometers and contained five million head of cattle or 33.3 per cent of the total cattle population of Colombia. The objectives of the program included the laying of a basis for disease eradication, the use of this area as a pilot project for the rest of the country, the elimination of the danger to Panama, and increased national livestock production. In addition to these objectives, the Colombians hoped to establish a basis for the export of livestock and livestock products and thus set an example for other countries faced with the FMD problem. The program in the north, however, proved expensive. Budget estimates ran to 23,974,000 pesos for 1967 and a total of 119,667,000 pesos for five years for all animal health problems. Of this sum, FMD programs received only 11,173,000 pesos for 1967 and 57,854,410 pesos for a five-year period.[15]

In view of the danger presented to the disease-free zone, Seoane and Palacios pointed out that "since Colombia has the greatest livestock potential of all the countries of the northern region of South America, . . . we placed special emphasis on the need to prepare and carry out the national control program and to conclude a treaty" with OIRSA. The program was accepted enthusiastically by Lleras Restrepo. In meetings with the Minister of Agriculture and his technical advisors, and representatives from stockraisers' associations, the importance of control programs, regional campaigns, and the use of external funds from the IDB were emphasized. Moreover, the vital role of the FMD Center was noted. Colombia, like most of the other Latin American countries, readily accepted its obligation for its annual share of support of the Center. The Center had already assisted Colombia through a consultant assigned there since 1964, an agreement for the administration of a modified live virus, a cooperative research program, an agreement with OIRSA (which was denounced by Colombia in 1966), and an agreement between Colombia, the Pan American Health Organization, and Ecuador to control FMD in the border areas.[16]

Ecuador

The spread of the malady seemed relentless in 1961, and Ecuador began its vaccination programs even before the presence of actual outbreaks in the country. Ecuadoran officials obtained immediate collaboration from civil, military, and ecclesiastical authorities in an attempt to convince the livestock raisers of the necessity of vaccinating their stock. In addition, information campaigns began, and information men, as in Mexico, were despatched to the different villages before vaccination brigades arrived.[17]

An autonomous agency for the fight against livestock maladies became a reality in February, 1961, when the Centro de Salud Pecuaria (Center of Agricultural Health) was established by Ecuadoran authorities. The new Center was financed by a tax on cattle and through external financial resources, principally monies from the AID. In addition, Ecuador remained concerned about its international commitments and consulted various international organs, especially the FMD Center.[18]

A problem with Colombia ensued, however, when in mid-1961, Colombian authorities announced the existence of Type A virus in the department of Nariño along the Colombo-Ecuadoran frontier. The Ecuadoran province of Carchi, which borders on Nariño, was at the time free of FMD. In November, Colombian technicians announced that Type O virus was also in the area, and probably because eradication measures were undertaken slowly, the infection reached the border by January, 1962. In response, Ecuador closed its border to livestock commerce and vaccinated all animals in Carchi in order to form a girdle of immune animals to protect the rest of the country. Meanwhile, uncontrolled human and animal traffic acted as ready though inadvertent carriers in the spread of the disease.[19]

Two meetings of the Consejo Nacional de Defensa Pecuaria (National Council of Agricultural Defense) in December, 1961, and February, 1962, attempted to come to grips with the problem that affected Colombo-Ecuadoran relations. The need for permanent vigilance in both Carchi and Nariño was emphasized, and a cattle census in Carchi and an intensified educational campaign were recommended. Preparation for a vaccination program began, and the Consejo Nacional asked for bank moratoria on loans from the National Development Bank and the Central Bank.[20]

Meanwhile, cattle movement in Carchi was restricted. With the exception of local movement, cattlemen in the area could not move their stock out of Carchi and were forced to undergo strict control measures even for local traffic. Vaccination plans began immediately on January 25, 1962, along the border. However, by February 5, the first outbreak was reported. The actual presence of FMD required a modification in plans, and rings of immunization were established in an attempt to circumscribe and inactivate the virus. Bivalent vaccine (Types A and O) was imported from the Instituto Zoöprofiláctico Colombiano at the rate of 25,000 doses a week. Another crisis developed, however, on February 7, when Ecuador ran out of vaccine as a result of a misunderstanding on vaccine orders between the Ecuadoran government and the Institute in Bogotá.[21]

Lack of vaccine was not the only impediment to the progress of the campaign. Ranches are scattered throughout the mountains and separated by great distances. Lack of modern facilities made the work uncomfortable, and often the only transportation available was by mule or horseback. Yet, the Ecuadoran brigades carried on their labors. Their efforts, however, failed to check the outbreak by February 5, and from that time to February 13 the malady occurred daily. Political difficulty arose on Febuary 13 when an outbreak occurred in an area where bivalent vaccine had been administered. Vigorous sanitary measures were immediately undertaken, but cattlemen in Ecuador were loathe to cooperate because they felt it was a Colombian problem. Meetings called by the government, however, informed them that malady had been introduced by clandestine cattle traffic across the border.[22]

With the mutual problem at hand, both Colombia and Ecuador readily recognized the international implications of the FMD outbreak along their borders, and the Ecuadoran Minister of Development wrote that "the isolated efforts that both countries are realizing will be of little avail if an integral campaign is not carried out in great proportions." Colombia responded and informed the Ecuadorans that the Ministry of Agriculture had kept in touch with the Centro de Salud Pecuaria. In addition, Colombia, in view of its international commitments, planned to inform Ecuador immediately of any outbreaks in Nariño, to report periodically on vaccination, to control the movement of susceptible stock and livestock products, to control and disinfect vehicles along the border, and to engage in an interchange of technical cooperation with Ecuador.[23]

Attempts to check the spread of the virus to the coastal regions failed, and numerous outbreaks of vesicular diseases, especially FMD, were prevalent in 1962. By September, Type A virus complicated the control and eradication program. Visits from members of the FMD Center staff coincided with outbreaks on the coast, and they approved the rigorous steps undertaken by the Ministry of Development in controlling the problem in Carchi and on the coast. Animal movement in Quito was strictly regulated, and vehicles were disinfected.[24]

Ecuador's experience necessitated the construction of a diagnostic and vaccine production laboratory. Initially, diagnoses were performed under far from auspicious circumstances without full collaboration by the Center in Rio. Makeshift equipment presented the main problem. However, according to the CSP, "diagnosis has been realized successfully, and part of the samples have been sent to outside laboratories, especially the Centro Panamericano de Fiebre Aftosa, and the results obtained have corresponded with those done in Ecuador." Ecuadoran efforts proved so apparently efficient that by the end of September, 1962, the Center asked that Ecuador train a Bolivian veterinarian in vesicular disease control. Thus, Dr. Jorge Aramayo, of Bolivia, received instruction and observed the work of the CSP in the control of FMD during October, November, and December, 1962.[25]

Relentlessly, the virus spread throughout Ecuador and by March, 1963, Types A and O appeared in Manabi, Guayas, Los Ríos, and El Oro. Meanwhile, Carchi, the original point of infection, was the center of intensive vaccination programs, along with Imbabura and Pichincha. Involved in the campaign were representatives of the FAO and the FMD Center. In all areas, vaccination consisted of three annual injections. In Carchi, especially, it was recommended that after the third injection, cattle receive a semi-annual vaccination.[26]

Simultaneously with its vaccination campaign, Ecuador began a building program to construct its Instituto Nacional de Diagnóstico y Producción de Vacunas (National Diagnostic and Vaccine Production Institute) in Guayaquil. By June, 1963, much of the laboratory was in use and facilitated the campaign. In part, the laboratory was financed through the auspices of the Pan-American FMD Center. Expense to Ecuador for the campaign during the first eighteen months amounted to $6,700,000, which included the purchase of equipment, vaccine, and the construction of the National Institute. With its new facilities, Ecuador felt prepared to manufacture an effective vaccine. Then, in July, 1963, the Ecuadoran government and the Pan American Sanitary Bureau signed an agreement to experiment with modified live virus vaccines. By August 29 the agreement was ratified, and experimentation with Type A virus, prevalent along the littoral provinces, began.[27] Ecuadoran efforts in the development of a modified live virus vaccine proved successful. The modified live virus produced by the National Institute showed 100 per cent innocuity in all experimentally vaccinated cattle. In addition, field trials of the vaccine also manifested the efficacy of the biologic.[28]

In response to the initial opposition to the anti-aftosa campaign in the first part of the program, Ecuador undertook an information program to facilitate the work of the brigades in the field in 1962–63. Ecuador's Ministry of Development stated that propaganda campaigns were "preliminary to whatever general type of socio-economic endeavor will have first priority in the future development of the campaign." [29] With this in mind, Ecuador established the Sección de Divulgación y Educación Sanitaria (Information Division) of the CSP with the cooperation of the Servicio Interamericano de Agricultura. A four-phase plan was initiated, including audiovisual demonstrations and lectures to cattlemen, distribution of illustrative materials, a widespread newspaper campaign, and demonstrations at cattle shows and fairs. Two sets of slide sequences were developed to show to cattlemen. Included in these series were explanations of methods of preventing vesicular diseases, ways in which cattlemen could cooperate with the authorities, and the technical means by which vesicular diseases were to be eradicated. In addition, interviews were taperecorded for use at cattlemen's meetings, especially in Carchi and Imbabura. Schools in Carchi also initiated basic courses in vesicular diseases so that students could readily recognize the symptoms of infection.[30]

It was not, however, until December, 1963, that Dr. Roberto Goíc, the FMD Center representative in Bogotá, was notified by the Ecuadorans of the outbreak along the Carchi-Nariño border. By the end of the month, an anti-aftosa meeting was held among representatives from Ecuador, Colombia, and the FMD Center. A tripartite program was initiated to eradicate the malady in Nariño and to control its spread in Ecuador. Renewed efforts in the area began almost immediately, and between early January and March, 1964, eight thousand doses of vaccine were administered in the region. The gravity of the threat presented by the Nariño outbreak and the arrangements made between the governments of Colombia and Ecuador along with the FMD Center prompted the signing of an agreement between Colombia, Ecuador, and the Pan American Sanitary Bureau in the fall of 1964.[31] Thus, three entities, two national and one international, joined in the anti-FMD battle. The details of the agreement provided for a reciprocal exchange of information, and the Colombian government was to notify Ecuador of any outbreaks in Nariño. Moreover, a mutual education campaign was to be initiated, and eradication and quarantine measures were to be established.[32] With the signing of the convention, the Ecuadoran Minister of Development ordered Ecuadoran adherence to the International Aftosa Convention, which had been drawn up in Bogotá between Panama, Venezuela, Colombia, and Ecuador in April, 1959.

Since the signing of the convention, Ecuador has maintained a livestock census in Carchi. Intensified efforts began in the control of all vesicular diseases, and movement of livestock and livestock products was reportedly controlled throughout 1965. By 1966, more equipment and personnel were added to intensify the program. Thus, Ecuador, despite her political problems in the 1960's, found that vigorous attention to the welfare of the national economy and the social problems that followed livestock disease and the resulting drop in food production transcended *cuartelazos* and domestic political quarrels.[33]

Peru and Bolivia

Continuing south along the Andean cordillera, Peru experienced serious waves of infection from all three virus types. Though aftosa had been known since 1910 and Peru had suffered a serious outbreak in 1944, the problem apparently was not widespread until the 1960's. By 1962–63, however, a massive outbreak of Type O struck near the Bolivian frontier causing losses estimated at 300 million *soles*. The Bolivian frontier was closed to commerce from Peru, but vaccination programs initiated by the Peruvian government were not comprehensive since only 35 per cent of the livestock was vaccinated during 1963.[34]

The new intensity of aftosa in Peru posed a potential threat to Ecuador's southern flank. As a result, the Peruvian Minister to Ecuador requested that anti-aftosa plans and materials be sent to the government of his country. In addition, Peru requested information from other afflicted South American countries. By September, 1963, the Peruvian government announced the formation of a Central Committee with administrative and economic autonomy and a budget of 28 million *soles*. It was obvious that Peru would be faced with economic disruption if the malady continued to spread. Within six months outbreaks of FMD in northern Peru made the threat to Ecuador more apparent, and on January 17, 1964, authorities from both countries met in Huaquillas, Ecuador, to discuss mutual problems in control and eradication of FMD. Both governments agreed to exchange data on outbreaks and to exchange professional observers during the course of their anti-aftosa campaigns. Moreover, mutual cooperation was agreed upon in the diagnosis of epithelial samples in the laboratories of Guayaquil and Lima.[35]

Peruvian efforts, despite Ecuadoran cooperation, had little effect, for vaccination was irregular, with less than 50 per cent of the livestock receiving vaccine in 1965 and 1966. The result was that about 60 per cent of the cattle remained unprotected should an epizoötic wave appear. By 1967 Peru had not yet begun a national anti-FMD campaign, and the Peruvian Minister of Agriculture, technicians, and representatives of the FMD Center gathered data for an application to the IDB for a loan. Primary in the proposed plan was the expansion of vaccine production laboratories, with $500,000 earmarked for that purpose from the IDB loan.[36]

Peruvian officials decided that the services rendered to Peru by the FMD Center deserved more financial aid than the amount stipulated in the agreement for support of the Center, and the Peruvian government budgeted $9,000 for Center support in its 1968 budget. From 1962 to 1967 the Center had kept a consultant in Peru, especially for help with laboratory installations. By early 1967, this consultant was replaced by one who was expert in field operations. Assistance in the preparation of inactivated virus vaccine and modified live virus vaccines also came from the Center, as well as help in the preparation of an IDB loan application. Significant aid also was provided in the coordination by the Center of the drafting of treaties between Peru, Ecuador, and the Pan American Sanitary Bureau, and between Peru, Bolivia, and the Sanitary Bureau for FMD prevention in the border areas.[37]

The Río de la Plata, Brazil, and Chile

During the years after World War II, the United States and Latin America have become increasingly aware of the international implications of livestock disease control. Working primarily through the Pan-American FMD Center, national and multinational groupings have coordinated their efforts to control and eventually eradicate livestock maladies such as foot-and-mouth disease. During the 1960's, the FMD Center served as the coordinating agency for various regional conferences that met to discuss the persistent aftosa problems that plague all of South America.

Argentina, Brazil, Chile, Uruguay, and Paraguay met at Montevideo at a conference convened by the FMD Center in February, 1962. Already aware of the projected epizoötiological survey of

Tierra del Fuego, the topic was placed on the agenda of the Argentine and Chilean delegations. It was agreed that the survey would cover all of Tierra del Fuego, and in March, 1962, an *ad hoc* FMD conference met in Washington at the National Academy of Sciences. At this time it was agreed that serological tests for presence or absence of the disease could be determined in that way. Both Chile and Argentina agreed to review their regulations for the movement of livestock from the island to the mainland, and procedures for reporting of communicable diseases every three months were established. Reports would go to the proper Chilean and Argentine authorities, the USDA, and the FMD Center. Additionally, the Center accepted the responsibility of statistical planning of the survey and the examination of serum samples.[38]

The Pan-American FMD Center

Throughout its existence, the FMD Center has operated on bare minimal budgets. It is financed in part through the Technical Assistance Program of the OAS. When the Inter-American Economic and Social Council met in Mexico City the FMD Center was continued and its finances renewed. In addition, the Center and US/AID signed an agreement that gave the former $237,000 for fiscal year 1963.[39] Monetary difficulties notwithstanding, the FMD Center expanded its national and international programs. Center consultants were permanently stationed in Rio de Janeiro, Bogotá, and Lima. The Bogotá consultant was charged with liaison in the Ecuadoran problem and the maintenance of vigilance between Venezuela and Colombia. In addition, he assisted Panama in its border quarantine to protect that country from infection that might emanate from Colombia. In connection with these consultants, other members of the Center staff were integrally involved in other consultative programs in 1963.[40]

Cognizant of its international responsibilities, the FMD Center encouraged and initiated the organization of regional groupings dedicated to an expansion of anti-aftosa programs to encompass regional objectives. The Comisión Regional de Sanidad Animal (Regional Commission on Animal Health) was created through ministerial decree in 1964 in Rio de Janeiro and coordinated by the Center. Comprising Chile, Argentina, Uruguay, Paraguay, and Brazil, in the so-called southern cone, the Regional Commission contacted various funding agencies in attempts to obtain external financing for its programs. Not all of its endeavors, however, proved successful until in April, 1965, the CIAP (Comité Interamericana, Alianza para el Progreso, or Inter-American Committee on the Alliance for Progress) announced that two agencies, the IDB and the International Reconstruction and Development Bank, were disposed to consider anti-FMD proposals. At the same time, the Pan American Sanitary Bureau strongly suggested that countries from the Regional Commission be given first priorities for monies in view of the chronic nature of their FMD problems.[41]

Border agreements to control the spread of FMD have been a principle concern of the Pan American Health Organization and its subsidiary agency, the FMD Center. Agreements between Colombia and Ecuador, Ecuador and Bolivia, and Peru and Bolivia have either been concluded or are under study. Such activity on the part of the FMD Center points to a constant interest in multinational approaches to FMD problems. The Regional Commission acted as a unifying factor in expanding and coordinating campaigns against FMD in the southern cone. At present, this group concerns itself with virus identification, vaccine control, certification of cattle for transit, and anti-aftosa campaigns. To give international scope to its program, all plans of action are meant to be essentially identical in countries belonging to the Regional Commission. One grouping brought about under Center auspices, however, has thus far failed—the Bolivarian Animal Health Organization, composed of Ecuador, Colombia, and Venezuela. Only Ecuador had ratified the Convention in 1967. The United States-Argentine Commission formed under Kennedy and Frondizi has continued its activities, and research programs have been initiated in Buenos Aires, the Pan American Center, and Plum Island.[42]

Probably one of the most effective regional groupings to date has been OIRSA (see Chapter V). With its regional offices in San Salvador, it collaborated with the Inter-American Institute for Agricultural Science in Costa Rica when it announced a sanitary cordon between Panama and Colombia of 25,000 square kilometers in an attempt to keep FMD out of the disease-free area. The Chocó region and the Darién area have formed a natural barrier against aftosa. The jungles, especially in Darién, have not been hospitable to livestock raising and have served as obstacles by which the virus might be deterred. However, extension of the Pan American Highway will open the area to greater danger of infection unless the most stringent sanitary measures are enforced.[43]

OIRSA and the Colombian government, moreover, entered into an agreement whereby Colombia would not use the Chocó for livestock raising, despite the economic potential of the area. By 1966, however, Colombia denounced the agreement, ostensibly because it could not economically buy stock from disease-free regions in order to develop adjacent areas. With the renunciation of the treaty in March, the fourteenth meeting of OIRSA in July approved the expansion of FMD control in the Darién area. Each OIRSA member country was levied an additional $15,000, for a total of $105,000, which included contributions from the Panamanian government and the Panamanian livestock growers. These additional monies allowed OIRSA to expand operations.[44]

Panama also responded unilaterally to the Colombian move and established a zone of 18,000 square kilometers in the Darién area where development of stockraising would be prohibited. Panamanian officials argued that this move would indirectly benefit most of the country through the protection afforded to the whole industry. A proposed treaty between OIRSA, Panama, Colombia, and the Pan American Sanitary Bureau would, in part, give compensation for such action. Seoane and Palacios further recommended that Colombia agree in the new treaty not to introduce animals into the Chocó and to undertake eradication measures as prescribed by the FMD Center. In addition, Colombia must carry out vigilant inspection in order to avoid the illicit traffic in animal products to Panama. At the same time, Central American countries and Panama were to agree to sell disease-free stock to Colombia at reduced prices to compensate for the Colombian sacrifice of not developing the Chocó. The governments could compensate the cattlemen for selling at reduced prices, and the transaction would be for one sale only with the number of head specified in the agreement. Further, the FMD Center recommended that the countries in the disease-free zone agree to carry out rigorous inspection at ports of entry and to establish stringent quarantines for vesicular disease, at least until laboratory diagnoses were made. In addition, in the unfortunate event of an outbreak of FMD, slaughter, inspection, and quarantine were to be used, with provisions for compensation for the cattlemen. Such agreements would delineate the measures taken in the defense of the unaffected area and the percentage of technical manpower and financial resources each country was to contribute.[45]

OIRSA members also initiated a program wherein each member country was to appoint a full-time veterinarian to deal exclusively with outbreaks of vesicular diseases. As of 1967, this aspect of the OIRSA operation has not been effective because of a paucity of transportation and financial resources. Yet, according to Seoane and Palacios:

> In our opinion, twelve years of experience show that OIRSA is doing an extremely important job. . . . As for the difficult tasks of preventing the introduction of foot-and-mouth disease into [the region], we believe that [OIRSA] must be endowed with sufficient technical and financial resources to allow it to accomplish this arduous task. We also believe that, in this connection, the advisory services of the . . . Center are essential.[46]

Ministers of Agriculture of the OIRSA countries prepared a cooperative FMD control program in consultation with the USDA and submitted it to U.S. Secretary of Agriculture Orville Freeman. In its totality, the objectives of the program were to keep the area free from disease through common regulatory arrangements, education programs, and investigations and diagnosis of laboratory specimens. When the OIRSA delegation delivered the program to Freeman in early 1967 they emphasized the importance of eradicating FMD in the hemisphere and underscored the necessity of regional cooperation in the interest of both domestic and foreign animal trade. Freeman responded that the USDA could not participate until Congress would pass enabling legislation, and he indicated that he would begin the process of getting a bill in Congress to allow this participation. In view of this, OIRSA chose to ask for monetary assistance from US/AID until the USDA could become an active participant.[47]

FMD Center specialists continue to give priority to the disease-free area. Specimens sent to São Bento are immediately analyzed and reports sent back at once. In addition to the consultant stationed in Panama, the Center has conducted eight training courses for regional veterinarians and has assisted OIRSA in some courses that it has sponsored. Thus, the FMD Center operated through regional groupings in an attempt to coordinate and make more efficient national and multinational programs.[48]

Central America, Mexico, and the Caribbean countries, according to Seoane and Palacios, stand to suffer potentially negative effects to their economies in proportion to the importance of livestock raising in their economic lives. "Furthermore," they continue, "the importance of import markets such as those of the United States must not be overlooked." In fact, an annual loss of $55 million was estimated for the unaffected areas through livestock deaths, reduced meat and milk production, and general livestock depreciation. The estimates did not include potential loss of revenue through a closure of the United States market should FMD strike the free zone.[49]

Central America and Panama, despite their concerted attempts to prevent FMD from entering the region, lack sufficient technical and financial resources to combat an outbreak of FMD. As a result, these countries, even with Panama's efforts to strengthen its defenses, have thus far failed to adopt all appropriate preventive measures. Central America and Panama have an extremely low number of veterinarians, averaging approximately one for each 90,000 head of livestock. When outbreaks of vesicular disease occur, quarantine measures are generally lax before a diagnosis is achieved, and transport for personnel is minimal. In addition, limited supervision and disinfection at roads, sea and airports, as well as untrained customs personnel, hinder preventive measures. In sum, if FMD were to appear in Panama or Central America, prompt eradication would be improbable, and an expensive and prolonged campaign could be anticipated.[50]

When the Inter-American Economic and Social Council met in Buenos Aires in March 1966, it approved a recommendation of the CIAP that the Secretariat prepare a report on the status of FMD in the hemisphere and the success of national campaigns to combat the malady. Moreover, it adopted recommendations about financing, and CIAP suggested that regular contributions be made from member countries with supplementary funds coming from public and private monies when available.[51] Yet, despite the many efforts in the 1960's, only limited advances in the control of foot-and-mouth disease were realized, and eradication appears to remain a far-off goal. A decade of economic travail and social instability in part hampered the successes of the various campaigns against the malady. At the same time, only in the very recent past have both international and national entities given FMD the priority necessary for successful eradication.

CHAPTER VIII

CONCLUSIONS

From the first appearance of aftosa in Latin America and the United States in the 1870's, the history of its effects on inter-American relations has demonstrated in microcosm the general trends extant in United States-Latin American relations and in the relations of one Latin American state with another. Strong regionalism, one of the basic characteristics of the vast territory south of the Río Grande, contributes to the nationalism of the countries within the region and has interfered with attempts to control or eradicate FMD. Vast mountains such as the Andes served to keep FMD out of Chile and the western part of South America for a period of time, but cross-regional traffic militated against the total immunity of western parts of the continent, and ultimately aftosa became a problem in the economies of all nations of the area. In contrast, the countries of the Río de la Plata were not aided by high mountains in keeping the disease out. The pampas readily allowed the malady to spread into

Uruguay, Paraguay, and Brazil so that by 1920 all areas suffered from the epizoötic.[1]

Political instability has also deterred campaigns against FMD. A tendency toward centralization and state action has, in the last half century, become more apparent in Latin America but has shown no notable success in combating FMD. Master plans such as the *Estado Novo* of Getúlio Vargas in Brazil, the *justicialismo* of Perón in Argentina, and the massive blueprint for social and economic better- ment of Mexico found in the Constitution of 1917 all point to greater and greater state participation in every facet of the economies and societies of Latin America. In the case of FMD, state action in Latin America has followed an erratic course, for the campaigns launched against the malady have been subject to the vicissitudes of political change, often abrupt and violent, that plague Latin America. Argen- tine authorities contend, for example, that compulsory vaccination, inspection, and rigid quarantine, and, if necessary, slaughter of ex- posed and infected stock, can only be carried out by the state in order to have a successful anti-aftosa campaign. Yet, Argentina has failed to eradicate the malady, partly as a result of its own unstable political situation.[2]

State action in the form of rigid plans has not kept Latin America free from FMD. The diverse populations of nearly all the Latin American republics where the disease has occurred have tended to make a strictly national approach highly problematical. Within each country marked ethnic and cultural differences and varying degrees of education and information demand primary consideration before any set program for eradication can be applied. Despite technical knowl- edge, legislation, and the practical necessity for eradication, anti- aftosa programs fail in their application without the cooperation of the farmers and cattlemen of the area. Opposition manifests itself in violent and passive forms, and where outright opponents do not exist ignorance and indifference limit the efficacy of control and eradica- tion procedures.[3]

In only one instance in Latin America has a vast, state-controlled program succeeded in the total eradication of FMD. When Mexico and the United States agreed to join forces against the malady, both were cognizant of the inherent threat to their reciprocal interests. Moreover, both countries adopted the agreement with dedication and the expressed intent of protecting their vital industries. Without the impending threat of infection it seems improbable that the United States would have joined Mexico in what soon became a successful eradication program. By 1946, Mexico had already experienced thirty-six years of revolutionary change in its political, economic, and social order. This transformation taught Mexican politicians the necessity of dealing with the various cultural groups within their nation. At the same time the United States participants in the eradication program became more aware of the different political and social customs to which they had to make necessary adaptations.

United States authorities, however, did not enter Mexico with a fanatical zeal to remake the society; rather, political differences were ultimately cast aside and vital mutual interests took precedence. To paraphrase Winston Churchill, the campaign was one of "blood, sweat, and tears," but the eventual conquest of aftosa in Mexico, despite high costs, including lives, finally convinced many Yankeephobes in Mexico of the sincere intent of the United States. As one authority at the time wrote, "the campaign in Mexico, in my opinion, is one of the largest cooperative programs in peacetime history and could serve as an example for the development of similar projects." [4]

Once aftosa was successfully eradicated from Mexican soil, both the United States and Mexico recognized the absolute necessity of maintaining continuing vigilance over their mutual livestock interests. CMAPPFA replaced CMAPEFA after 1954 and became a mutual commitment of both governments. When Seoane and Palacios visited Mexico in March, 1967, they viewed their trip as extremely important because of the web of commercial relations between Mexico and its Central and North American neighbors. Moreover, Mexico, having experienced and successfully eradicated FMD, and having overcome the social and other problems inherent in such a program, could serve as an example to the rest of the hemisphere of the necessity of realistically effective cooperation among the republics of the New World. Mexican authorities, aware of their international obligations, have supported plans proposed by the FMD Center for regional and hemispheric action in the prevention and elimination of aftosa. Mexico, however, failed to give a written commitment as to its financial support of the FMD Center because of uncertainty concerning the contribution in relation to its overall obligation to the OAS.[5]

Immediately after visiting Mexico, Seoane and Palacios traveled north to the United States and reported to Pan American Health Organization authorities and USDA officials on the results of their talks with governments of the inter-American system. In their report, they detailed the status of anti-aftosa campaigns in South America, the unique position of Colombia because it borders on the disease-free area, and the necessity of a treaty between Colombia and its northern neighbors. Of primary importance, they stressed the need of appreciating the human, technical, and economic resources of all of the countries in Latin America in order to combat more effectively the malady that plagues the greater part of the hemisphere. As exponents of the role of regional cooperation, Seoane and Palacios underscored the importance of the FMD Center and the desirability of providing that agency with "adequate and permanent financing" beginning in 1968.[6]

United States officials were disappointed, however, by the failure to develop concerted preventive action in the Caribbean and the West Indies or the coordination of national plans. Seoane and Palacios noted that the "southern cone" countries, as well as Ecuador, Venezuela, and Colombia were effectively coordinating their plans and that Peru and Bolivia were about to enter into a cooperative effort to eradicate the malady. Moveover, they noted, a special mission from the Pan American Sanitary Bureau would be dispatched to the Caribbean.[7]

At a meeting with Dr. Lincoln Gordon, Assistant Secretary of State for Latin American Affairs, and State Department members and representatives from the OAS and its specialized agencies, Seoane and Palacios presented the same report they have given to the USDA and the Pan American Health Organization. Gordon thought the proposals resulting from the visits to the Latin American countries excellent and raised no objection to the 66 per cent quota the United States was asked to contribute to the support of the FMD Center, provided other countries paid their allotted shares. He did indicate, however, that the proposal for the Center would have to be presented in such a way that it could be handled under existing administrative procedures. Fear was expressed that if more administrative agencies were created, Congressional approval of support might prove difficult. Apparently, more than a few congressmen feared the growth of more bureaucratic machinery within what they considered an already bloated inter-American complex.[8]

Even though State Department and USDA officials tentatively approved programs proposed by Seoane and Palacios, Congressional approval, at this writing, has not yet come, and the history of United States attitudes on programs to combat FMD in Latin America might yet act as a brake on effective United States participation in a concerted hemispheric effort to eradicate the malady. Pressures exerted from livestock owners in the United States, as well as conviction on the part of the BAI, kept the United States from embarking on a potentially detrimental course when it signed the Sanitary Convention with Argentina in 1935. As Bryce Wood indicated, the Good Neighbor Policy had its limitations when priorities inimical to national interests took precedence in the eyes of some policy makers. Section 306 (a) of the Smoot-Hawley Tariff Act of 1930 was clearly intended to protect the United States livestock industry from competition from South America. But at the same time, and despite what some called purely nationalistic economic motivation, it equally served to protect United States livestock from infection from FMD countries.[9]

War and cold war forced the United States to turn away from its Latin American neighbors and to give slight consideration to the social, economic, and political problems, partly the result of wartime propaganda and economic dislocations, of its southern partners. Only in the case of Mexico did the United States lend wholehearted support to FMD eradication, and Mexico benefited from that liberal display of enlightened self-interest on the part of the United States. Revolutionary ferment continued in Latin America throughout the 1950's and with the initiation of the Alliance for Progress in 1961 a supposedly new remedy for Latin America was proposed by President Kennedy. Again, however, the aim somehow fell short of the mark. Pressures continued to mount in Latin America for an amelioration of economic and social problems, but the United States' responses seemed jaded.

United States action on foot-and-mouth disease in Latin America did become more vigorous when the government was subjected to domestic pressures. Proximity to Mexico dictated an active interest in the presence of aftosa in that country. The appearance of FMD in Mexico posed a direct threat to United States livestock interests, for the virus could easily have swept across the border and infected livestock in the United States with disease. Also, for cattlemen in the Southwest livestock from northern Mexico was a source of feeder cattle, and the closure of the border between 1946 and 1954 was a factor in the reduction of Southwestern beef production during those years.

Despite the interest manifested toward Mexico, the United States has been slow to cooperate in FMD eradication in the Río de la Plata region and elsewhere in South America. Conversations with USDA officials indicate that a division of opinion exists in the United States as to whether or not aftosa can even be eradicated in South America. Those who argue against involvement point out that the disease is so thoroughly diffused in Argentina and Uruguay, for example, that it would be impracticable to attempt to eradicate it. Also, the United States is not contiguous to South America and not directly threatened by infection if strict sanitary regulations are not followed. Implicit in this opinion is the fear, often not articulated, of competition from low-priced, high-quality meat. Though comparative statistics on prices of United States and South American meat were not available, it can be surmised that the almost exclusively range production methods of a pastoral country such as Argentina, combined with a lower labor cost, would effectively force United States producers to cut prices in order to compete with imported meat. Livestock interests in the United States, as already indicated, pressured their congressmen and senators to vote against legislation or international agreements that might facilitate cooperation between the United States and Latin America in FMD eradication or liberalize restrictions on trade of livestock and livestock products.

Potentially threatening social and political problems in Latin America probably prompted Kennedy to acquiesce in Frondizi's wish to reinvestigate the possibility of importing meat from Patagonia and Tierra del Fuego to the United States, despite scientific findings that rendered such a proposal dangerous to the United States. United States veterinarians, represented by the American Veterinary Medical

Association, lauded the initiation of short- and long-term research projects on FMD but perceptively noted that "were there no political forces at work," no long-term project would have been born so quickly. In addition, it was constantly emphasized by scientists that scientific, not political, realities must have precedence in order to protect the United States livestock industry from possible contamination. Again, international political considerations overrode national priorities when the United States Chief Executive acted positively on Frondizi's request, for subsequent events in 1967 clearly showed the danger of importing meat from Tierra del Fuego.[10]

Next to Western Europe, the United States was the largest purchaser of South American meat and meat products, particularly salt-cured beef, which was imported in the amount of 21,500 tons valued at $9,800,000. Yet, all statistics fail to show that the income of Latin America has been channeled into such social benefits as roads, schools, industrial development in general, and the improvement of nutritional standards. This situation led IAECOSOC to declare that "the economic and social aspects of the livestock industry are but two sides of the same problem." Reduction of livestock production and its domestic and foreign commerce "will have detrimental consequences for the socio-economic situation in the Latin American countries." [11] In short, insufficient commerce, both domestically and internationally, will ultimately work against Latin America.

Greater attempts at economic integration in Latin America— demonstrated by the Latin American Free Trade Association and the Central American Common Market—presage the necessity for United States involvement in regional efforts to combat aftosa if it wishes to remain an integral part of the economic life of the Western Hemisphere. Both the free and infected areas, in view of regional trends toward economic integration, must confront the FMD menace from a hemispheric point of view if the New World wishes to limit dependence on Asia and Europe. Increasing integration may even produce new factors that could make control and eradication more difficult. The Pan American Highway, for example, will greatly assist transit from one country to another but at the same time will more readily contribute to possible spread of the disease. Therefore, it becomes incumbent upon the members of the inter-American system to work efficiently and rapidly to remove ultimately the livestock plague from its lands.[12]

Latin America still shows a distinct reluctance to use the "sanitary rifle" in its eradication procedures, even though heavy reliance upon vaccination has thus far failed to eliminate, or even to substantially control, the malady. Yet, the necessity of not destroying the subsistence economies of many rural dwellers in Latin America remains. Again, Mexico and the United States showed that a modified slaughter program buttressed by vaccination not only eradicated aftosa, but also eliminated some inferior stock from Mexico. A subsequent program of livestock improvement raised the general quality of Mexican animals. Similar programs could be applied in other Latin American countries with due consideration of differences in geography, culture, economic potential, and political development and organization.

The Alliance for Progress, has, unfortunately, failed to take into account the differences in culture and historical development that distinguish Latin American countries from the United States and from each other. Emphasis on political and economic reform predicated on narrow, preconceived notions may ultimately work against a solution of fundamental problems such as food shortages and nutritional deficiencies. The formation of the Joint Argentine-United States Commission on Foot-and-Mouth Disease indicated some cognizance of the value of technical assistance programs without concern for political and social differences on the part of Kennedy and his advisors. Foot-and-mouth disease, writes one food technologist,

> is a problem that involves the United States in its relationships with all of South America. By helping all of our neighbors south of the border to help themselves via a scientific Alliance for Progress, the United States, as a world leader, can contribute directly, on a people-to-people basis, to the economic development of these nations. Training of students, exchanges of faculty in food science and technology, and research as a multidisciplinary approach of the virologist, the veterinarian, and the food scientist will help open new export markets, enlarge existing ones and, in the long run, help solve one of the most important economic epizootic diseases.[13]

No country in the Western Hemisphere, with the possible exceptions of the United States and Canada, can successfully defeat FMD on the basis of its own resources alone. Regional cooperation, coordinated by the FMD Center and the Pan American Health Organization, seems to be the only practicable solution to the resolution of the

FMD problem in the hemisphere. The so-called population explosion in Latin America is creating a growing food problem, and the elimination of FMD would help ameliorate a tendency toward famine. OAS action through an increased technical assistance program may lead to the final elimination of aftosa. At this writing, the "need to mount a continent-wide program to control the disease makes it essential to ensure adequate financial support for the Pan American Foot-and-Mouth Disease Center."[14]

Concerted regional efforts to eradicate aftosa are hindered by the threat of irrational nationalism that occasionally leans toward xenophobia. National fears, prejudices, and jealousies intrude upon and hinder hemispheric cooperation. The United States and Latin America equally share blame for narrowness in their respective approaches to social and economic problems such as foot-and-mouth disease. United States emphasis on the defeat of the Communist threat in the hemisphere forces it into the uncompromising position of demanding a decision between a democratic government and communistic forms of government in Latin America. At the same time, Latin Americans often react irrationally to United States attempts to help as merely another attempt of Yankee imperialism to keep them under control. Argentine reactions, for example, to United States quarantines clearly show a one-sided simplistic interpretation of United States motives for restricting livestock trade with all of South America.

Thus, technical assistance, freed from the impediments of political harangues and recriminations, seems the most feasible approach to a resolution of a hemisphere-wide problem. The national interests of North America and Latin America, remain at stake. Concerted action, much like that in which Mexico and the United States entered twenty years ago, offers the most feasible solution to the elimination of aftosa and the development of unity in the Western Hemisphere.

POSTSCRIPT

Since the initial writing of this manuscript, events in Latin America, England, and the United States require the addition of a postscript to the book. Probably beginning in late 1966 or in the first month of 1967, foot-and-mouth disease struck again in England. The disease mounted in intensity until it was estimated that approximately 250,000 head of livestock would perish from the sanitary rifle. United States newspapers and television newscasts carried the grim news during the peak of the infection (Fall, 1967). England, meanwhile, struggled with its eradication problem and at the same time attempted to ascertain the source of infection. Educated guesses about the origin of the malady placed it in either Argentina or Uruguay, two of England's largest suppliers of export meat.

With the outbreak in the British Isles, United States veterinary officials manifested due concern with the possibility of an introduction of FMD into the United States. Especially noticeable was their worry over tourists acting as carriers of the disease when traveling in Europe and then returning home. In New York State, for example, the State Department of Agriculture circulated vast amounts of literature to veterinarians in the state in an attempt to apprise them of the incipient danger. My own veterinarian had posters prominently displayed warning his clients of the danger and advising them on how to best guard against the introduction of the disease.

Of equal importance to the Western Hemisphere were two other occurrences that were recently reported to me by Dr. Frank J. Mulhern of the Agricultural Research Service, USDA. According to Dr. Mulhern, the House of Representatives introduced a bill that would enable the Secretary of Agriculture to ally the United States with regional groups dedicated to the deterrence of animal and plant contagion. This is especially significant in that in all probability the impetus for this came from the recent meeting of OIRSA representatives with Secretary of Agriculture Orville Freeman. With the Central American concern for the maintenance of that area as a zone free of FMD, the introduction of the technical skills of the United States into the preventive struggle enhances the likelihood of keeping the area north of Chocó in Colombia free of infection.

The second event of equal consequence for United States-Latin American cooperation in the control of aftosa was a meeting in Washington in the Spring of 1968 of the Ministers and Secretaries of Agriculture of the Western Hemisphere to report on their progress in the control of vesicular diseases and especially aftosa. As yet, the official report of the meeting has not been prepared, but it should be noted that these meetings will be an annual occurrence. The next one is scheduled to be in Rio de Janeiro in 1969.

The coincidental convergence of the three events—the outbreak in England, the introduction into the House of Representatives of enabling legislation, and the meeting in Washington—makes clear a growing preoccupation with foot-and-mouth disease as more than a national problem. It therefore becomes incumbent upon the United States to grasp the leadership of a massive international effort to eradicate aftosa in the Western Hemisphere. To do this, however, the United States needs to realign its international priorities in terms of aid and commitment.

When James G. Blaine as Secretary of State called the first Pan

American Conference in 1889 he envisioned an economic *Zollverein* consisting of the United States and Latin America. As yet, this has failed to materialize. The United States and Latin America have gone their separate ways in many respects and the last fifty years have shown that Blaine's ideal has remained but a dream. Yet, worldwide developments practically mandate that the United States join its Latin American neighbors in some sort of economic union. Europe's common market is, for all intents and purposes, closed to the United States; most of Asia and Africa are unstable, which militates against high economic production by either domestic or foreign interests. Latin America already contains the highest amount of United States investment capital outside of the United States, but xenophobic Latin American nationalists thunder against "imperialism" from north of the Río Grande. At the same time, more moderate nationalists rightfully point out that the tariffs in the United States are often imposed more for economic protectionist motives than for revenue or sanitary protection. The Smoot-Hawley Tariff Act of 1930 is a case in point.

It would be folly, however, for the United States to lift its tariff barriers to livestock from infected countries at this time. To achieve the Pan American ideal of free trade within the hemisphere, however, the United States must take the lead in the elimination of the causes of those barriers. Latin America, too, has its responsibility in the reduction of obstacles to trade, for countries such as Peru and Bolivia, which lack many of the natural resources for full industrialization, need to concentrate on those things they are best equipped to produce. Tariff agreements, the Latin American Free Trade Association, the Central American Common Market, and increased participation by all members of the OAS in the eradication of FMD will remove another impediment to free trade within the hemisphere.

Though it is not the function of the historian *qua* historian to recommend policy and to gaze longingly into the future, he should, especially when dealing with modern history, make his work applicable to the present. Therefore, it would seem that the United States should: 1) increase its efforts in cooperative FMD control in the hemisphere; 2) reorient its policies from political display (such as the Alliance for Progress) to more active and long-lasting bases for inter-American cooperation; 3) stand firm in the face of demands for a relaxation of provisions that protect the interest of the United States in terms of sanitary conventions, tariffs, and executive orders until such time as lowering them would not jeopardize the livestock industry in this country; and 4) join with the other American republics in the elimination of the causes (such as FMD) of the tariffs and executive orders that hinder free trade in the hemisphere and impede harmonious relations.

Dallas, Texas
September 1968

Manuel A. Machado, Jr.

APPENDIXES

APPENDIX A

DISTRIBUTION OF THE BUDGET OF
THE PAN AMERICAN FOOT-AND-MOUTH DISEASE
CENTER IN ACCORDANCE WITH THE QUOTA
SCALE OF PAN AMERICAN UNION

Country	Percentage	Contribution in $
Argentina	7.11	85,522
Bolivia	.31	3,729
Brazil	7.34	88,288
Chile	2.09	25,139
Colombia	1.78	21,410
Costa Rica	.31	3,729
Cuba	1.54	18,524
Dominican Republic	.31	3,729
Ecuador	.39	4,691
El Salvador	.31	3,729
Guatemala	.31	3,729
Haiti	.31	3,729
Honduras	.31	3,729
Mexico	6.26	75,297
Nicaragua	.31	3,729
Panama	.31	3,729
Paraguay	.31	3,729
Peru	.69	8,299
United States	66.00	793,872
Uruguay	.77	9,262
Venezuela	2.93	35,242
	100.00	$1,202,836.00

SOURCE: Seoane-Palacios, *Report,* Annex 1(A).

APPENDIX B

TREATY SERIES, NO. 808

CONVENTION
Between
THE UNITED STATES AND MEXICO

Safeguarding Livestock Interests
Through the Prevention of Infectious
and Contagious Diseases

Signed at Washington, March 16, 1928
Ratification Advised By The Senate, March 28, 1928 (Legislative Day of March 27, 1928)
Ratified by The President, April 7, 1928
Ratified by Mexico, December 13, 1929
Ratifications Exchanged At Washington, January 17, 1930
Proclaimed, January 18, 1930

By The President
Of The United States Of America

A PROCLAMATION

WHEREAS a convention between the United States of America and the United Mexican States to safeguard the live stock interests of their respective countries through the prevention of the introduction of infectious and contagious diseases was concluded and signed by their respective Plenipotentiaries at Washington on the sixteenth day of March, one thousand nine hundred and twenty-eight, the original of which Convention, being in the English and Spanish languages, is word for word as follows:

The Government of the United States of America and the Government of the United Mexican States, being desirous to safeguard more effectually the live stock interests of their respective countries through the prevention of the introduction of infectious and contagious diseases, have, for that purpose, agreed to conclude a Convention, and have to that end appointed as their respective plenipotentiaries:

The President of the United States of America, Frank B. Kellogg, Secretary of State of the United States of America; and

The President of the United Mexican States, His Excellency Señor Don Manuel C. Téllez, Ambassador Extraordinary and Plenipotentiary of the United Mexican States at Washington;

Who, having exhibited to each other their respective full powers, which were found to be in good and due form, have agreed upon the following Articles:

ARTICLE I

The High Contracting Parties agree to maintain at designated border and sea ports authorized for the importation of animals an adequate live stock sanitary police service to guard against the introduction of animals affected with or exposed to contagious disease, and to notify each other at least ten days in advance whenever a port is to be closed or a new one is to be opened. In case of live stock imported or in bond the official veterinary inspectors of either country are authorized to make inspections, supervise dippings, and apply the necessary tests upon either side of the border as may be convenient.

ARTICLE II

Quarantine stations shall be maintained by the High Contracting Parties at designated border and sea ports for animals imported from foreign countries. Such animals shall be kept under observation and subjected to tuberculin, mallein, blood, or other tests as may be necessary for the diagnosis of disease.

ARTICLE III

The High Contracting Parties agree to supervise the sanitary handling of animal by-products, forage, and other commodities offered for importation that may be carriers of infectious and contagious diseases and to prohibit the importation of forage or other articles accompanying live stock affected with such diseases or suspected of being so affected.

ARTICLE IV

The appropriate authorities of each of the High Contracting Parties shall incorporate in their regulations the necessary measures governing the disinfection of vessels and all kinds of vehicles used in the transportation of animals and of the quarantine stations or other premises occupied by animals affected with dangerously acute and rapidly spreading contagious diseases such as foot-and-mouth disease, rinderpest, contagious pleuropneumonia, and hog-cholera.

ARTICLE V

The competent officials of each of the High Contracting Parties shall prescribe the form and requirements of the permit and certificates to be presented as evidence that the animals are eligible for importation; of the manifests, bill of lading and other papers to be submitted by importers, captains of vessels, or others in charge of live stock offered for importation; and of the records to be kept by the veterinary officials at the ports of entry.

ARTICLE VI

The form and requirements of certificates which shall accompany shipments of animal by-products, hay, straw, and other imported commodities shall be specified by the duly authorized officials of each of the High Contracting Parties.

ARTICLE VII

It is agreed that an efficient veterinary live stock sanitary police service shall be maintained under the Department of Agriculture in the United States and the Secretaria de Agricultura y Fomento in Mexico to combat infectious, contagious, or parasitic diseases of live stock.

ARTICLE VIII

The live stock sanitary officials shall define the specific territory in their respective countries in which any contagious or infectious disease exists and shall indicate zones which may be considered as exposed, in order to prevent the propagation and dissemination of the infection of such disease.

ARTICLE IX

The High Contracting Parties shall not issue permits for domestic ruminants or swine originating in any foreign countries or zones where highly infectious and rapidly spreading diseases such as foot-and-mouth disease and rinderpest appear frequently, until at least sixty days have elapsed without any outbreak of the disease in such countries or zones. When a disease of this kind occurs in any part of a foreign country any other part of the same country shall be considered as exposed until the contrary is positively shown, that is, until it is shown that no communication exists between the two parts by which the disease may be readily transmitted. When such a disease occurs near the land border of a foreign country the neighboring part of the adjacent country shall be considered as exposed until the contrary is positively shown.

ARTICLE X

It is agreed that the respective governments shall notify each other promptly, through the usual diplomatic channels, of the appearance and extent of seriously acute, contagious diseases. In the case of outbreaks of diseases of this character not recently existing in either country information may be transmitted immediately in the most expeditious manner.

ARTICLE XI

The High Contracting Parties agree to exchange the official regulations, periodicals, and other publications that may come out in their countries on the subject matter of this Convention and information concerning changes and substitutions which may be developed in the methods of prophylaxis, control, and care of animal diseases; and also to establish an interchange of students and experts and visits of representatives of the respective governments, for the purpose of studying and observing on the ground methods of control and eradication of such diseases as may break out in the territory of either of the nations.

ARTICLE XII

Special regulations shall be issued by each of the High Contracting Parties governing the movement of live stock between the respective countries. These regulations shall specify in each case the veterinary sanitary police measures applicable.

ARTICLE XIII

Certificates of inspection and testing of live stock, issued by duly authorized veterinarians of either country, shall be accepted as proof that such inspection and testing have been made; but, in any case of the offer of live stock for importation into either country, the issuance of such certificate shall not preclude further tests of such animals, or further investigation with respect thereto, to determine their freedom from or exposure to disease, before entry is permitted.

ARTICLE XIV

This Convention shall be ratified, and the ratifications exchanged at the city of Washington as soon as possible.

The Convention shall come into effect at the date of publication in conformity with the laws of the High Contracting Parties, and it shall remain in force until thirty days after either party shall have given notice to the other of a desire to terminate the Convention.

In WITNESS WHEREOF, they have signed the present Convention and have affixed thereto their respective seals.

Done in duplicate, in the English and Spanish languages, at the City of Washington, this sixteenth day of March, one thousand nine hundred and twenty-eight.

FRANK B KELLOGG (Seal)

MANUEL C. TÉLLEZ (Seal)

AND WHEREAS the said Convention has been duly ratified on both parts, and the ratifications of the two Governments were exchanged in the city of Washington on the seventeenth day of January, one thousand nine hundred and thirty;

NOW, THEREFORE, be it known that I, Herbert Hoover, President of the United States of America, have caused the said Convention to be made public, to the end that the same and every article and clause thereof may be observed and fulfilled with good faith by the United States and the citizens thereof.

IN TESTIMONY WHEREOF, I have hereunto set my hand and caused the seal of the United States to be affixed.

DONE at the city of Washington this eighteenth day of January in the year of our Lord one thousand nine hundred and thirty, and of the Independence of the United States of America the one hundred and fifty-fourth.

HERBERT HOOVER

By the President:

JP Cotton
Acting Secretary of State

SOURCE: [First] *Senate Report.*

APPENDIX C

CONVENTION WITH ARGENTINA WITH REFERENCE TO SANITARY REGULATIONS CONCERNING PLANT AND ANIMAL PRODUCTS

MESSAGE
FROM
THE PRESIDENT OF THE UNITED STATES
TRANSMITTING

A Convention Between The United States Of America and The Republic Of Argentina With Reference to Sanitary Regulations Concerning Plant and Animal Products, Signed At Washington May 24, 1935

June 5, 1935.—Convention read the first time and referred to the Committee on Foreign Relations, and, together with message, ordered to be printed in confidence for the use of the Senate.

To The Senate of the United States:
   With a view to obtaining the advice and consent of the Senate to the ratification thereof, I transmit herewith a convention between the United States of America and the Republic of Argentina with reference to sanitary regulations concerning plant and animal products. The agreement is described and explained in the accompanying report of the Secretary of State, to which the Senate's attention is invited.
   The purpose of entering into this convention is to establish cooperation in the prevention of the introduction and spread of infectious and contagious plant and animal diseases and insect pests and to facilitate the visits and studies of Government experts engaged in surveys in regard to these matters. The interests of this Government are fully protected in article III which reserves to the respective governments the right to prohibit importations from any territories or zones which it finds to be affected with or exposed to contagion or infestation.

The same article provides that neither country may prohibit the importation of products from territories of the other, which it finds to be not affected or exposed to such contagion or infestation, because diseases or pests exist in other territories or zones. This provision operates to prevent the use of sanitary regulations as a disguised means of restriction of importations for protective purposes, and accordingly fulfills as between the United States and Argentina Resolution No. XXVIII of the Fourth Pan American Commercial Conference, held in Washington in October 1931.

The convention also provides for consultation as to the application of sanitary laws and regulations and for the establishment of a committee of experts, in the event of disputes as to sanitary regulations, with power to submit recommendations to the two Governments.

In view of all of the foregoing considerations, I believe this convention to be highly desirable, and I ask the Senate to advise and consent to its ratification in the interest of trade and good understanding between the two countries.

FRANKLIN D. ROOSEVELT.

(Accompaniments: Convention; Report of the Secretary of State.)
THE WHITE HOUSE, June 5, 1935.

THE PRESIDENT:

I have the honor to send you herewith a convention between the United States of America and the Republic of Argentina with respect to sanitary regulations concerning plant and animal products, signed at Washington, May 24, 1935. This convention has been signed, in accordance with the full power issued by you, subject to ratification, and accordingly it is sent to you with a view to transmission to the Senate for the purpose of receiving the advice and consent of that body to its ratification, if you approve thereof.

This convention formulates measures of cooperation between the two Governments toward the accomplishment of their mutual desire to prevent the introduction and spread of infectious and contagious plant and animal diseases and insect pests.

Article I provides for prompt notification by each Government to the other Government of the appearance and extent of plant and animal diseases and insect pests, dangerous to human, animal, or plant life.

Article II provides for the exchange of official and scientific information. It permits, and requires the facilitation of, visits of experts of the Government of one country engaged in studying and observing the existence, distribution, and methods of control and eradication of diseases and pests in the territory of the other country.

Article III provides that each party recognizes the right of the importing country to prohibit the importation of animal or plant products originating in or coming from territories or zones which it considers to be affected with or exposed to plant or animal diseases or insect pests. That article also provides that neither country may prohibit importations from territories or zones in the other country which it finds to be free from, and not exposed, to, contagion or infestation for the reason that diseases or pests exist in other territories or zones.

This article of the convention will fulfill as between the United States and Argentina Resolution No. XXVIII adopted by the Fourth Pan American Commercial Conference held in Washington in October 1931, which reads as follows:

> The Fourth Pan American Commercial Conference Resolves:
> 1. To acknowledge as fundamental principles that sanitary police regulations effective at the present time, or enacted in the future to regulate the inter-American traffic of vegetable and animal products, must not have in their practical application the character of protective customs measures.
> 2. That in the application of all restrictions of a sanitary nature in the inter-American traffic of animal and vegetable products, in order to determine the origin of the product, the term "infected zones" be used instead of "infected countries"; upon condition that the country of origin give all necessary facilities to determine its sanitary condition.
> 3. To recommend to the American countries the negotiation of agreements for the regulation of the foregoing principles.

Article IV of the convention provides that certificates of origin of inspection of plant and animal products issued by the appropriate officers of either country shall be accepted as proof of such origin or inspection; but such certificates do not preclude further investigation or inspection by the importing country.

Article V provides for consultation with respect to the application of sanitary laws and regulations. In the event of disagreement as to the application of such laws and regulations, this article provides that a committee of technical experts shall be constituted to consider the matter and make recommendations to the two Governments. Provision is also made for consultation prior to the application of any new sanitary measure.

The approval of this convention will do much toward strengthening friendly intercourse between the United States and Argentina, and will place their relations with respect to sanitary laws and regulations upon a just and scientific basis, without impairing the sovereign right of either Government to impose sanitary measures deemed necessary in its judgment for the protection of its livestock and agricultural interests.

Respectfully submitted.

CORDELL HULL.

(Enclosure: Convention.)
DEPARTMENT OF STATE,
   Washington, June 4, 1935.

The United States of America and the Republic of Argentina, being desirous of cooperating to prevent the introduction and spread of infectious and contagious plant and animal diseases and of insect pests, have agreed to conclude a convention for that purpose, and have appointed as their respective plenipotentiaries:

The President of the United States of America: Mr. Cordell Hull, Secretary of State of the United States of America;

The President of the Republic of Argentina: His Excellency Dr. Felipe A. Espil, Ambassador Extraordinary and Plentipotentiary of the Republic of Argentina at Washington;

Who, having communicated to each other their respective full powers, found to be in good and due form, have agreed upon the following articles:

ARTICLE I

The Government of the United States of America and the Government of the Republic of Argentina will notify each other promptly, through the usual diplomatic channels, of the appearance and extent of plant and animal diseases and of insect pests dangerous to human, animal, or plant life.

ARTICLE II

The two contracting Governments will exchange the official regulations, periodicals, and other publications that may be issued in the respective countries on the subject-matter of this convention and likewise information concerning changes and substitutions which may be developed in the methods of prophylaxis, control, and care of plant and animal diseases and insect pests.

ARTICLE III

Each contracting party recognizes the right of the other party to prohibit the importation of animal or plant products, originating in or coming from territories or zones which the importing country considers to be affected with or exposed to plant or animal diseases or insect pests dangerous to plant, animal, or human life, until it has been proved to the satisfaction of the party exercising such right that such territory or zone of the party is free from such contagion or infestation or exposure to contagion or infestation. Neither contracting party may prohibit the importation of animal or plant products originating in and coming from territories or zones of the other country which the importing country finds to be free from animal or plant diseases or insect pests or from exposure to such diseases or pests, for the reason that such diseases or pests exist in other territories or zones of the other country.

ARTICLE IV

Certificates of origin or inspection of plant and animal products, issued by duly authorized sanitary officials of either of the contracting countries, shall be accepted by the authorities of the other country as proof of such certificates by the authorities of one of the contracting countries shall not preclude further inspection of the products by the authorities of the other country, or further investigation with respect to them, to determine their freedom from infection or infestation or exposure to disease or insect pests, before entry is permitted.

ARTICLE V

The Government of the United States of America or the Government of the Republic of Argentina, as the case may be, will accord sympathetic consideration to such representations as the other Government may make regarding the application of sanitary laws and regulations for the protection of human, animal, or plant life.

In the event that the Government of either of the contracting countries makes representations to the Government of the other country in respect of the application of any sanitary law or regulation for the protection of human, animal, or plant life, and if there is disagreement with respect thereto, a committee of technical experts on which each contracting Government will be represented shall, on the request of either Government, be established to consider the matter and to submit recommendations to the two Governments.

Whenever practicable each Government, before applying any new measure of a sanitary character, will consult with the Government of the other county with a view to insuring that there will be as little injury to the commerce of the latter country as may be consistent with the purpose of the proposed measure. The provisions of this paragraph do not apply to actions affecting individual shipments under sanitary measures already in effect or to actions based on pure food and drug laws.

ARTICLE VI

This convention shall be ratified and the ratifications shall be exchanged at the city of Washington as soon as possible.

The convention shall come into force on the day of exchange of ratifications and shall remain in force until sixty days after either contracting party shall have given notice to the other party of its intention to terminate the convention.

In witness whereof the respective plenipotentiaries have signed the present convention and have affixed thereto their seals.

Done in duplicate, in the English and Spanish languages, at the city of Washington this twenty-fourth day of May in the year of our Lord one thousand nine hundred and thirty-five.

CORDELL HULL (Seal)
FELIPE A. ESPIL (Seal)

NOTES

Preface

1. Maurice S. Shahan, "Foot-and-Mouth Disease: One of the most important of Infections of Animals," *American Cattle Producer* (March, 1952), p. 10, hereafter cited as Shahan, "FMD."

2. *Report on Foot-and-Mouth Disease: Present and Future Problems on the American Continent and the Importance of the Pan American Foot-and Mouth Disease Center,* Mission: Edgardo Seoane and Carlos Palacios (Washington, D.C.), 1967, pp. 1–2, hereafter cited as Seoane and Palacios, *Report.*

3. Félix Humberto Paiva. *La Fiebre Aftosa en Números: Severo Impacto en la Economía Pecuaria Latino-Americana,* p. 4, hereafter cited as Paiva, *Aftosa en Números.*

4. Inter American Economic and Social Council, "The Economic Importance of Foot-and-Mouth Disease in the Americas," *Second Annual Meeting of the Inter American Economic and Social Council at the Expert Level and at the Ministerial Level, October–November 1963. Sao Paulo, Brazil* (Washington, D.C., October, 1963), pp. 2, 9, hereafter cited as IAECOSOC.

5. "Foot-and-Mouth Disease Breaks Out in Canada," *Journal of the American Veterinary Medical Association* (April, 1952), p. 185, hereafter the journal will be cited as *JAVMA;* A. W. Miller, "Foot-and-Mouth Disease in the United States," *Year Book of Agriculture, 1926* (Washington, D.C., 1926), p. 378.

Chapter I

1. Secretaría de Agricultura y Ganadería, *Instituto de la Fiebre Aftosa* (Buenos Aires, n.d.), pp. 8–9, hereafter cited as Secretaría, *Instituto;* C. Griffin, *Fiebre Aftosa,* pp. 1–18; República Argentina: Secretaría de Estado de Agricultura y Ganadería de la Nación, Dirección General de Sanidad Animal, Servicio de Luchas Sanitarias (SELSA), *Antecedentes Cronológicos de la lucha Contra la Fiebre Aftosa* (limited circulation manuscript), hereafter cited as SELSA, *Antecedentes.* All of the above provide background information for the early history of aftosa in Argentina.

2. State Department Papers, Record Group 59, 611.3556/27, United States Legation in Buenos Aires to Secretary of State, July 29, 1910. Hereafter only the file number and the author-recipient will be cited.

3. 611.3556/47, William H. Robertson to Secretary of State, August 29, 1916.

4. 835.607k/a, Department of State to United States Consul-General at Buenos Aires, June 2, 1920; 835.607k/1, United States Consul General at Buenos Aires to Department of State, June 4, 1920.

5. Secretaría, *Instituto,* p. 7.

6. SELSA, *Antecedentes.*

7. 611.355/59, Thaw to Morgan, Department of State, Division of Latin American Affairs, July 9, 1927; 611.355/40, Secretary of Agriculture to Secretary of State, July 18, 1927.

8. E. Louise Peffer, "Foot-and-Mouth Disease in United States Policy," (Stanford University) *Food Research Institute Studies* (May, 1962), p. 151, hereafter cited as Peffer, "FMD in U.S. Policy." A more negative view of United States quarantines can be found in Arthur P. Whitaker. *The United States and Argentina,* p. 144, hereafter cited as Whitaker, *U.S and Argentina;* 641.355/2, Robert Woods Bliss to Secretary of State, January, 1928.

9. 711.35/53, Robert Woods Bliss to Secretary of State, January 26, 1928.

10. 103.8/348, Robert Woods Bliss to Secretary of State, October 30, 1928.

11. J. N. Ritchie, "Foot-and-Mouth Disease in South America," *The Journal of the Ministry of Agriculture and Fisheries* (November, 1959), p. 323, hereafter cited as Ritchie, "FMD in South America."

12. Peffer, "FMD in U.S. Policy," pp. 142–43; *Report of the Delegates of the United States of America to the Sixth International Conference of American States, Habana, Cuba, January 16 to February 20, 1928* (Washington, D.C., 1928), p. 260.

13. Peffer, "FMD in U.S. Policy," pp. 160–1.

14. SELSA, *Antecendentes.*

15. Peffer, "FMD in U.S. Policy," pp. 154–5; it has been noted that since the outbreak in Los Angeles strict sanitary regulations with regard to meat importations have kept the United States free of aftosa. Shahan, "FMD," pp. 10–11.

16. 611.0056/40, Memorandum from the Division of Latin American Affairs, April 24, 1929.

17. Peffer, "FMD in U.S. Policy," pp. 44–5, 157–60.

18. *Ibid.,* pp. 142, 155–6; *Congressional Record,* 71st Congress, First Session, September 12, 1929, pp. 3568–9.

19. 611.3556/78, Argentine Ambassador to Secretary of State, June 18, 1931, and Orme Wilson to Mr. Thurston, Memorandum, June 20, 1931.

20. 611.3556/84, State Department Legal Advisor, Memorandum, September 28, 1931.

21. 611.3556/86, J. C. White, Counselor of Embassy, Buenos Aires, to Secretary of State, October 14, 1931.

22. Peffer, "FMD in U.S. Policy," p. 143.

23. 611.3556/87, Felipe Espil to Francis White, October 26, 1931; 611.3556/91, Espil to Secretary of State, November 11, 1931; 611.3556/85, E. C. Wilson to Mr. White, October 26, 1931; 611.3556/95, J. C. White, Charge de Affaires, Buenos Aires, to Secretary of State, November 21, 1931.

24. 311.3556/99, J. C. White to Secretary of State, January 22, 1932; 611.3556/100, Orme Wilson, Memorandum on Conference with Dr. S. O. Fladness, January 29, 1932.

25. Peffer, "FMD in U.S. Policy," pp. 163–94; Whitaker, *U.S. and Argentina,* p. 44.

26. All information in this section on Mexico is derived from Manuel A. Machado, Jr., *"Aftosa* and the Mexican-United States Sanitary Convention of 1928," *Agricultural History* (October, 1965), pp. 240–45.

27. *Ibid.,* pp. 240–1.

28. *Ibid.,* pp. 241–2.

29. *Ibid.,* pp. 242–3.

30. *Ibid.,* pp. 243–4.

31. *Ibid.,* p. 244.

32. U.S. Department of State, Treaty Series 808, "Convention between the United States and Mexico: Safeguarding Livestock Interests through the Prevention of Infectious and Contagious Diseases," as published in (California) Senate Interim Committee on Livestock Diseases. *Report on Foot-and-Mouth Disease* (Sacramento, 1948), pp. 209–17. This report and two others (1949, 1951) offer excellent source materials for a study of FMD in Mexico and will be cited subsequently as [First, Second or Third] California *Senate Report,* respectively.

33. 611.2356, Secretary of Agriculture to Secretary of State, December 15, 1923; 611.2356/1, Consulate General in Lima to Secretary of State, February 4, 1924.

34. 825.6222. This entire file gives a detailed description of the general decline of the Chilean cattle industry as a result of Argentine livestock imports; Chile. Consejo Superior de Hijiene. *La Fiebre Aftosa del Ganado* (Santiago, 1910), *passim.*

35. 611.2556/13, Republic of Chile, Ministry of Foreign Affairs, Copy of Dispatch regarding Foot-and-Mouth Disease Inspection attached to Chilean Foreign Minister's Letter of March 9, 1924; 611.2556/10, R. W. Dunlap, Acting Secretary of Agriculture to Secretary of State, August 15, 1930; 611.2556/9, Thomas S. Horn, Consul at Antofagasta to Secretary of State, January 25, 1930.

36. 611.3356/, Consul at Montevideo to Secretary of State, June 28, 1910; 611.3356/2, Consul at Montevideo to Secretary of State, July 9, 1910, 611.3356/3, Consul at Montevideo to Secretary of State, August 15, 1910.

37. 611.325, United States Consul at Montevideo to Secretary of State, April 22, 1918.

38. 611.3356/9, U. Grant Smith, United States Legation in Montevideo to Secretary of State, November 29, 1927.

39. Lourenço Granato. *A Febre Aphtosa,* pp. 1–6, and *passim;* 611.3556/17, Vice Consul General at Rio de Janeiro to Secretary of State, June 20, 1910; 611.3556/13, Consul at Pará to Secretary of State, June 21, 1910.

40. 611.3256/1, Consul at Pernambuco to Secretary of State, January 7, 1919; 611.3256/4, Secretary of Agriculture to Secretary of State, January 21, 1919; 611.3256, United States Consul at Pernambuco to Secretary of State, September 22, 1916.

41. 611.3256/14, Consul at Porto Alegre to Secretary of State, July 21, 1919; 611.3256/16, Consul at Porto Alegre to Secretary of State, August 16, 1919.

42. 611.325/7, Henry C. Wallace, Secretary of Agriculture, to Secretary of State, July 28, 1922, and Department of State to Consul at Rio de Janeiro, August 1, 1922.

43. 611.325/9, Henry C. Wallace to Secretary of State, August 21, 1922.

44. 611.325/14, Division of Latin American Affairs to Mr. White, June 28, 1923.

45. 611.3256/20, Consul General at Rio de Janeiro to Secretary of State, August 7, 1923; 611,325/14, C. V. Marvin, Acting Secretary of Agriculture, to Secretary of State, November 2, 1923; Congressman Claude B. Hudspeth to Matthew Hanna, Head, Mexican Division, Department of State, April 7, 1924.

46. 611.0056/10, Count Fernand de Lusino to Secretary of State, October 21, 1924; 611.0056/11, Secretary of Agriculture to Secretary of State, n.d.; 611.0056/13, Consulate at Porto Alegre to Secretary of State, December, 1924.

Chapter II

1. Bryce Wood, "The Department of State and the Non-National Interest: The Cases of Argentine Meat and Paraguayan Tea," *Inter-American Economic Affairs* (Autumn, 1961), pp. 4, 6, hereafter cited as Wood, "Department of State."

2. 641.3515/19, Robert Woods Bliss to Secretary of State, March 17, 1933; 611.355/103, Orme Wilson, Division of Latin American Affairs, conversation with Mr. Maudlin of the Bureau of Applied

Economics, June 3, 1933; 611.3556/107, Felipe Espil to Cordell Hull, Secretary of State, June 22, 1933, and E. Wilson (Division of Latin American Affairs) to Secretary of State, June 28, 1933.

3. Wood, "Department of State," pp. 6–7.

4. 611.355/13, Spruille Braden to Cordell Hull, January 1, 1934.

5. 611.3556/120, Vice Consul in Buenos Aires to Department of State, December 19, 1934.

6. 611.355/125, Translation from *La Nación,* March 21, 1953; 711.359, Division of Latin American Affairs to Mr. Wilson, April 24, 1935.

7. Wood, "Department of State," pp. 6–7; 711.359/4A, Cordell Hull to Franklin D. Roosevelt, n.d., and Roosevelt to U.S. Senate, n.d.

8. 711.359/5, Ambassador Alexander Weddell to Secretary of State, May 31, 1935.

9. 711.359, *passim;* Wood, "Department of State," p. 12.

10. 711.359/8, E. P. Thomas, President, National Foreign Trade Council, to Cordell Hull, May 31, 1935.

11. Wood, "Department of State," pp. 6, 13.

12. 711.359/27, Alexander Weddell to Secretary of State, June 25, 1935, enclosing a translation from *El Diario* (Buenos Aires), June 23, 1935, and *La Prensa* (Buenos Aires), June 24, 1935; 711.359/44, Weddell to Secretary of State, July 5, 1935.

13. Voluminous protests from senators and congressmen can be found in 611.3556/107; 711.359/42, Josh Lee, Representative from Oklahoma, Fifth District, to Cordell Hull, July 12, 1935. It should be noted that Lee was himself a cattleman; Wood, "Department of State, p. 14.

14. *Ibid.,* pp. 12–13; 711.359/64, Consul General A. M. Warren, Buenos Aires, to Secretary of State, July 19, 1935.

15. *Congressional Record,* 74th Congress, First Session, August 9, 1935, pp. 12806–12807.

16. F. E. Mollin, "The Necessity for Rigid Sanitary Embargoes in Combating Foot-and-Mouth Disease," *American Cattle Producer* (December, 1935), pp. 11–17.

17. 811.001—Roosevelt Visit/285, Alexander Weddell to Secretary of State, n.d.; 710. Peace/11, Weddell to Sumner Welles, February 6, 1936; 611.3531/382, Memorandum of Conversation with Argentine Informant, Weddell to Secretary of State, April 17, 1936; 611.3551, Consul at Buenos Aires to Lawrence Duggan, Chief, Division of American Republics, June 15, 1938.

18. 611.423 cattle/131, Francis B. Sayre (State Department) to Albert K. Mitchell, President, American National Livestock Association, April 25, 1936.

19. "La Fiebre Aftosa y Nuestro Comercio de Carnes con el

Reino Unido," *Revista de Medicina Veterinaria* (July, 1936), pp. 444–5.

20. *Congressional Record,* 75th Congress, First Session, February 5, 1937, pp. 906–7.

21. *American Cattle Producer* (June, 1937), pp. 9–10; 611.3531 /529, Memorandum of Conversation between F. B. Sayre and Felipe Espil, October 1, 1937.

22. By 1941, the Argentine decree was modified with the establishment of a one-week quarantine before animals could enter the southern territories and the Sección Veterinaria Patagonia (Patagonia Veterinary Section) was created. SELSA, *Antecedentes;* Wood, "Department of State," pp. 19–20; 711.359—Sanitary/443, Lawrence Duggan to Sumner Welles, Cordell Hull, and Francis Sayre, February 4, 1938; 611.355/162, Memorandum of conversation between Miguel E. Querino-La Valle, Commercial Attaché, Argentine Embassy; Carlos García Mata, United States Representative of the Cooperative Organization of Argentine Packinghouses; and Mr. Stinebower (State Department), n.d. These last-mentioned Argentines, cognizant of the failure of the Department of State to achieve treaty ratification, suggested the appointment of a United States Commission to study the Argentine aftosa problem.

23. 611.355, *passim;* 611.353/743, Monnet B. Davis, Consul-General, Buenos Aires, to Secretary of State, February 6, 1939; 611.355/167, Argentine Embassy to Department of State, February 13, 1939.

24. 611.3531/1754, Cordell Hull to Representative A. T. Treadway (Massachusetts), March 6, 1939; James E. Poole, "Persistent Argentina Seeks Our Market," *American Cattle Producer* (April, 1939), p. 34.

25. *Congressional Record,* 76th Congress, First Session, May 15, 1939, pp. 5526–7, 5530–35, 5538; 611.355/196, Harry L. Brown, Acting Secretary of Agriculture, to Secretary of State, May 4, 1939; *El Comercio* (Lima), May 20, 1939, as found in 510.1131/243; Louis G. Dreyfus, Jr., Chargé d'Affaires, Lima, to Secretary of State, May 21, 1939; 611.355/207, Monnet Davis, Consul General, Buenos Aires, to Secretary of State, July 17, 1939; *Buenos Aires Herald* as cited in *Congressional Record,* 76th Congress, First Session, Appendix, August 1, 1939, p. A3754; 611.355/220, M. L. Wilson, Acting Secretary of Agriculture, to Secretary of State, December 19, 1939.

26. Peffer, "FMD in U.S. Policy," p. 143.

27. U.S. Department of State, *Foreign Relations of the United States. The American Republics 1940* (Washington, D.C., 1957), Vol. V, Argentine Embassy to Department of State, p. 508, hereafter cited as Department of State, *Foreign Relations.*

28. *American Cattle Producer* (January, 1941), p. 16, and (March, 1941), p. 26; Department of State, *Foreign Relations 1935,* Vol. IV, p. 296; Wood, "Department of State," p. 23.

29. Jacob Traum and H. W. Schoening, "Report on a Visit to Foot-and-Mouth Disease Institutes in South America," unpublished manuscript supplied to the author by Dr. Raymond Bankowski, School of Veterinary Medicine, University of California, Davis, California, pp. 30–42, hereafter cited as Traum and Schoening, "Report."

30. John W. White. *Argentina: The Life Story of a Nation,* p. 195, hereafter cited as White, *Argentina.*

31. 611.355/253, Memorandum from Harry C. Hawkins, Division of Commercial Treaties and Agreements, Department of State, March 29, 1941; *La Nación* as quoted in *New York Times,* April 17, 1941.

32. Felix J. Weil. *Argentine Riddle,* pp. 200–201, hereafter cited as Weil, *Argentine Riddle.*

33. 711.359 Sanitary/511, United States Embassy, Buenos Aires, to Secretary of State, June 18, 1941.

34. 611.355/269, United States Embassy, Buenos Aires, to Department of State, August 14, 1941.

35. 611.355/280, L. A. Wheeler, Director, USDA, Office of Foreign Agricultural Relations, to United States Embassy, Buenos Aires, October 24, 1941.

36. *The New York Times,* January 9, 1942.

37. Weil, *Argentine Riddle,* pp. 201–2.

38. 611.3556/150, United States Embassy, Buenos Aires, to Secretary of State, June 9, 1943.

39. Argentina. Dirección de Sanidad Animal. *Lucha Contra la Fiebre Aftosa, passim.*

40. SELSA, *Antecendentes.*

41. *The New York Times,* June 25, 1945.

42. 711.359/67, Consul General at Montevideo to Secretary of State, July 19, 1935.

43. 611.335/42, Legation at Montevideo to Secretary of State, December 11, 1936; *El Diario* (Montevideo) October 11, 1937, as found in 611.3331/124, L. E. Reed, Charge de Affaires, Montevideo, to Secretary of State, October 13, 1927.

44. 611.3356/19, S. O. Fladness to Department of State, October 9, 1942.

45. 611.3356/20, Joel Hudson, Assistant Commercial Attaché, United States Embassy, Montevideo, to Secretary of State, October 24, 1942; 611.3356/21, R. G. Glover, Commercial Attaché, Montevideo, to Secretary of State, May 15, 1943.

46. 611.3256, George J. Haering, United States Consul in Per-

nambuco, to Secretary of State, June 11, 1934, August 6, 1934, and October 1, 1934; 611.3256/32, Haering to Secretary of State, May 12, 1936; 611.325/29, Rexford G. Tugwell to Secretary of State, May 28, 1936.

47. J. Elmer Brock, "Some Observations on a South American Trip," *American Cattle Producer* (August 1941), pp. 5–6.

48. 611.2556/16, Tugwell to Secretary of State, December 31, 1934; 611.2556/17, Tugwell to Secretary of State, July 19, 1934.

49. 611.2556/18, Camden L. McLain, United States Vice Consul, Santiago, to USDA, August 25, 1936; 611.2556/20, Consul at Santiago to Secretary of State, March 15, 1940; 611.2556/23, James Parker Wilson, Agricultural Economist, U.S. Embassy, Chile, to Secretary of State, June 12, 1942.

50. 611.2556/23, James Parker Wilson to Secretary of State, June 12, 1942.

51. 611.2556/24, United States Ambassador to Chile to Secretary of State, December 1, 1942.

52. 611.2456/1 U.S. Legation, La Paz, Bolivia, to Secretary of State, March 12, 1943.

53. Ecuador. Dirección General de Ganadería y Veterinaria. *La Fiebre Aftosa en el Ecuador. Informe Oficial* (Quito, 1961), Mimeograph, p. 1, hereafter cited as *La Fiebre Aftosa en Ecuador, 1961.*

Chapter III

1. For a detailed study of Mexican-United States cooperation in aftosa control see Manuel A. Machado, Jr., *An Industry in Crisis; Mexican-United States Cooperation in the Control of Foot-and-Mouth Disease;* Guillermo Quesada Bravo. *La Verdad Sobre el Ganado Cebu Brasileño. La Fiebre Aftosa y la Cuarentena en la Isla de Sacrificios,* pp. 49–50, 31–35, hereafter cited as Quesada Bravo, *La Verdad;* Mervin G. Smith, "The Mexican Beef Cattle Industry," *Foreign Agriculture* (November, 1944), p. 254; *Agriculture in the Americas* (September, 1944), p. 162; James A. Porter. *Doctor, Spare My Cow,* p. viii, hereafter cited as Porter, *Doctor.* All of the above works provide detailed information on the problem about the bulls.

2. Marte R. Gómez, "The Truth about the Brahmans, Speculations on Foot-and-Mouth Disease," [Third] California *Senate Report,* pp. 102–103, hereafter cited as Gómez, "Truth."

3. *Ibid.,* pp. 112–13, 114, 121, 123, 124–30, 138–40, 148–50, and *passim; Excelsior* (Mexico City), June 3, 1946; R. E. Seltzer and T. M. Stubblefield. *Marketing Mexican Cattle in the United States, passim.*

4. Gómez, "Truth," pp. 150, 160–61, 164–5; "Joint Mexican-United States Veterinary Commission Report in Relation to Cattle

Imported From Brazil," October 16, 1946, [First] California *Senate Report*, pp. 327–8; *Dallas Morning News*, [First] California *Senate Report*, p. 346.

5. Gómez, "Truth," *passim;* Quesada Bravo, *La Verdad, passim;* also see *El Universal* (Mexico City), June 18, 20, and 22, 1946, and *Excelsior*, August 30, September 1 and 3, 1946.

6. Gómez, "Truth," pp. 166–7.

7. Statement of Paul J. Revely, Acting Chief, Division of Mexican Affairs, Department of State. *Eradication of Foot-and-Mouth Disease. Hearings before a Subcommittee of the Committee of Agriculture*, House of Representatives, 80th Congress, First Session, December 3, 4, and 5, 1947 (Washington, D.C., 1948), p. 143, hereafter cited as *House Hearings*.

8. Oscar Flores, "Remarks to the California Senate," March 9, 1950, [Third] California *Senate Report*, p. 33; USDA, *Farmer's Bulletin #666*, "Foot-and-Mouth Disease" (Washington, D.C., 1952), pp. 4–5; Drs. Federico Rubio Lozano, Fernando Camargo, César Clavell, M. S. Shahan, H. F. Kern, and A. E. Wardlow to the Mixed Mexican-United States Agricultural Commission, January 24, 1947, private archive of Dr. Fernando Camargo Núñez, cited hereafter as Camargo Archive; Comisión contra la Fiebre Aftosa. *La Fiebre Aftosa en México* (México, D.F., 1951), pp. 4, 11, 15, hereafter cited as Comisión *La Fiebre Aftosa;* Interview with Dr. Fernando Camargo Núñez, June 25, 1962, hereafter cited as Camargo Interview; *El Universal*, December 30, 1946, provides a good example of the newspaper coverage given to the closure of the border to Mexican stock.

9. *El Universal*, January 10, 1947.

10. Fernando Camargo *et al.* to the animal industry subcommission of the Mexican-United States Agricultural Commission, January 8, 1947, library of the Dirección General de Investigaciones Pecuarias, Palo Alto, D. F., hereafter cited as Palo Alto Library; Open letter from Oscar Flores in *Excelsior,* October 25, 1947; Camargo Interview; Ramón Auró Saldaña. *Factores que han influído en la Extensión y la Propagación de la Fiebre Aftosa en Nuestro País,* p. 22, hereafter cited as Auró Saldaña, *Factores;* Comisión, *La Fiebre Aftosa,* pp. 15, 22, 27.

11. Comandancia Militar de la campaña contra la Fiebre Aftosa, Estado Mayor, March 15, 1947, Palo Alto Library.

12. See issues of *Excelsior, El Universal,* and *Ultimas Noticias* (Mexico City) for details on the formation of the *juntas municipales* and the state committees.

13. Comisión, *La Fiebre Aftosa,* pp. 16, 22, 27; Camargo Interview; *El Universal,* January 5, 9, and 11, 1947.

14. *Congressional Record,* 80th Congress, First Session. See the

proceedings of both houses in the early months of the session, and specifically the *Record* of February 21, 1947; *El Universal*, February 25, March 1, 7, and 30, 1947; John A. Hopkins, "Fight Against Foot-and-Mouth Disease in Mexico," *Agriculture in the Americas* (June–July, 1947), p. 96, hereafter cited as Hopkins, "Foot-and-Mouth Disease;" Copy of an American Broadcasting Company Interview with Don Stoops, USDA Attaché, United States Embassy, Mexico City, April 5, 1947, Camargo Archives; Comisión, *La Fiebre Aftosa*, p. 15; United States Department of State. *Treaties and other International Acts, Series 2404, Eradication of Foot-and-Mouth Disease in Mexico* (Washington, D.C., 1953), pp. 6–8, hereafter cited as *TIAB 2404;* USDA, Agricultural Research Administration, March 11, 1947, [First] California *Senate Report,* p. 383, hereafter cited as Ag. Research Ad.

15. Hopkins, "Foot-and-Mouth Disease," p. 96; USDA, *Farmer's Bulletin #666,* p. 10; Dirección General de Ganadería, Reglamento, May 7, 1947, Palo Alto Library. All of these spell out in detail restrictions on livestock movement.

16. *Excelsior,* February 14, 1947; Comisión, *La Fiebre Aftosa,* pp. 15–16; *El Universal,* January 2, 1947; American Broadcasting Company Interview with Oscar Flores, April 5, 1947, Camargo Archives, hereafter cited as ABC Interview with Flores; Statement of B. T. Simms, BAI Director, *House Hearings,* p. 2; Camargo Interview; Statement of General Charles H. Corlett, retired, Special Representative of the Secretary of Agriculture, *House Hearings,* p. 29.

17. *Novedades* (Mexico City), January 3, 1948.

18. Camargo *et al.* to subcommission of the Mexican-United States Mixed Agricultural Commission, January 24, 1947, Camargo Archives; Simms Statement, *House Hearings,* pp. 15, 18, and *passim; Excelsior,* October 13, 1947.

19. Fred Gipson and Bill Leftwich. *The "Cow Killers:" With the Aftosa Commission in Mexico,* p. 33.

20. *El Universal,* January 6, 1947; Meeting of CMAPEFA, Minutes, May 6 and 7, 1947, and July 30, 1947, Camargo Archives; *Excelsior,* October 13, 22, and 28, 1947; *House Hearings,* p. 89 and *passim.*

21. *Novedades,* January 10, 1948.

22. Statement of Charles W. Wiswall, *House Hearings,* pp. 61–63; USDA, Ag. Research Ad., March 18, 1948, [Second] California *Senate Report,* p. 36; [Third] California *Senate Report,* p. 9; *Novedades,* January 12, 1948.

23. Tape-recorded interview with Dr. Robert J. Schroeder, Los Angeles County Livestock Department Director, and Mr. Cecil Lewis, USDA, September 11, 1961, hereafter cited as Schroeder-Lewis Interview.

24. *El Universal,* October 9, 1947; *Novedades,* January 10, 1948.

25. USDA, Ag. Research Ad., July 23, 1947, August 4, 1947, [First] California *Senate Report,* pp. 395, 401; *Excelsior,* September 24 and 26, 1947; USDA, Ag. Research Ad., April 26, 1947, CMAPEFA Meeting, Minutes, May 6 and 7, 1947, Camargo Archives.

26. *Excelsior,* June 25 and September 22, 1947; CMAPEFA Meeting, July 30, 1947, Camargo Archives; B. T. Simms, "Change in the Foot-and-Mouth Disease Program," December 3, 1947, Camargo Archives, announces the change from the all-out slaughter program to the modified slaughter and vaccine phase of the eradication program; *El Universal,* October 9, 1947.

27. *Excelsior,* October 11, 18, and 22, 1947.

28. Simms Statement, Clarkson Statement, and Corlett Statement, *House Hearings,* pp. 3, 38, 50–51 respectively.

29. Comisión, *La Fiebre Aftosa,* p. 31; CMAPEFA Meeting, November 27, 1947, and Ceremonia de la Creación del Consejo Consultivo para la Preparación de la Vacuna Anti-aftosa, January 12, 1948, hereafter cited as Ceremonia, Camargo Archives; Corlett Statement, *House Hearings,* p. 58; Simms, "Changes in the FMD Program," Camargo Archives; [Third] California *Senate Report,* p. 8.

30. *El Universal* and *Excelsior,* September 25, 1947; H. F. Wilkins, Committee of the United States Livestock Sanitary Association, "Report on Foot-and-Mouth Disease," [Third] California *Senate Report,* p. 31; Comisión, *La Fiebre Aftosa,* p. 23; Ceremonia, Camargo Archives.

31. Consejo Consultivo Meeting, January 23 and 27, 1948, CMAPEFA, *Boletín de Prensa,* January 21, 1948, Camargo to Oscar Flores, February 8, 1948, Camargo Archives.

32. USDA, Ag. Research Ad., May 10, 1948, October 29, 1948, and February 7, 1949, [Second] California *Senate Report,* pp. 30, 40, 50, respectively; Drs. C. R. Omer and C. A. Manthei to Flores and Shahan, June 1, 1948, Camargo Archives.

33. George Kirksey, Special Representative, Joint Livestock Committee, Chicago, Illinois, "Report" of June 10, 1949, [Third] California *Senate Report,* p. 47, hereafter cited as Kirksey, "Report;" Ag. Research Ad., July 29 and September 1, 1949, [Third] California *Senate Report,* pp. 48, 55–6; Camargo Interview.

34. Comisión, *La Fiebre Aftosa,* pp. 35–6, 42, 61, 69; Camargo Interview; *Nuevo Plan para la Erradicación de la Fiebre Aftosa,* Camargos Archives.

Chapter IV

1. *Congressional Record,* 80th Congress, Second Session, April 7, 1948, p. 4195 and p. A1028.

2. USDA, Ag. Research Ad., June 15 and October 20, 1948, [Second] California *Senate Report,* pp. 70–72, 43; *Novedades,* January 8, 1948, describes the location and construction of the disinfection tanks.

3. *Novedades,* January 9, 1948.

4. USDA, Ag. Research Ad., July 5, 1950, [Third] California *Senate Report,* p. 83.

5. Kirksey, "Report" of June 10, 1949, [Third] California *Senate Report,* p. 47.

6. USDA, Ag. Research Ad., May 12, 1949, in *ibid.,* p. 38.

7. *Ibid.,* May 16, 1949, p. 39.

8. *Ibid.,* October 25, November 2, and December 12, 1949, and March 29, 1950, pp. 59, 61, 69, and 74, respectively.

9. Kirksey, "Report" of March 9, and July 10, 1950, in *ibid.,* pp. 76–7; Information Division, CMAPEFA, March 9, 1950, in *ibid.,* p. 36; *Excelsior,* February 3, 1950; Asociación Nacional de Productores de Leche Pura to Oscar Flores, November 4, 1950, Camargo Archives.

10. R. J. Anderson, Director, Division of Animal Disease Eradication, USDA, to author, July 11, 1961; Interview with Dr. Luis de la Torre Zarza, Comisión México-Americana para la Prevención de la Fiebre Aftosa, June 25, 1963, hereafter cited as De la Torre Interview.

11. De la Torre Interview; *Excelsior,* May 24 and 25, 1953.

12. De la Torre Interview.

13. Simms and Corlett Statements, *House Hearings,* pp. 5–6, 53; Schroeder-Lewis Interview.

14. Comisión, *La Fiebre Aftosa,* pp. 29–30; Porter, *Doctor,* pp. 16–18; USDA, Ag. Research Ad., May 12, 1949, [Third] California *Senate Report,* p. 29; Schroeder-Lewis Interview.

15. *Excelsior,* October 23, 1947.

16. Kirksey, "Report" of July 11, 1949, [Third] California *Senate Report,* p. 51; Porter, *Doctor,* pp. 16–18; USDA, Ag. Research Ad., May 12, 1949, [Third] California *Senate Report,* p. 29.

17. For a thorough discussion of religion in Mexico, see Nathan L. Whetten. *Rural Mexico,* Chapter 19; Kirksey, "Report" of March 9, 1950, [Third] California *Senate Report,* p. 77.

18. De la Torre Interview; Oscar Lewis, *Children of Sánchez,* p. 197.

19. *Excelsior,* June 17, 1947.

20. *Ibid.,* September 4, 19, 20, 22, 27, October 3, 9, and 31, 1947; *La Prensa* (Mexico City), October 8, 1947; *El Universal,* October 9, 1947; USDA, Ag. Research Ad., September 20, 1947, [First] California *Senate Report,* p. 412; De la Torre Interview.

21. USDA, Ag. Research Ad., February 7, 1949, [Second] California *Senate Report,* pp. 48–9; *Excelsior,* February 7, 1950.

22. *Excelsior,* June 10, 1947.

23. Simms Statement, *House Hearings,* pp. 6–7; *Excelsior,* September 24, 1947. The poem in *Excelsior* translates as follows: Whichever aftosa-infected beef the sanitary rifle cures/shall no longer get sick/of that malady./That can be assured./Now in Mexico/it can be seen as a sad truth/that the remedy/has been worse than the cure./Our cattle are killed without compassion/only for the protection/of the neighbor's stock./If aftosa spreads there/the neighboring cattleman/would lose money/while he combated it./And if it does not spread there, understand,/that those well-paid people/will become richer selling/hides and canned milk./Thus, if the neighbor helps, it is only for his own good/and the people begin to doubt/who is helping who?/For that reason, if that exotic vaccine is successful/ to suspend the slaughter/would be a patriotic labor./Even though it's better late than never/it would be an opportune thing/to defend our bovine richness/with vaccine./

24. Conference on Vaccine Production, January 3, 1948, Camargo Archives; Clarkson Statement, *House Hearings,* p. 29; Kirksey, "Report" of August 10, 1949, [Third] California *Senate Report,* pp. 54–5.

25. Auró Saldaña, *Factores,* pp. 27–8.

26. Corlett Statement and Statement of Albert K. Mitchell, *House Hearings,* pp. 49, 66–7.

27. *Excelsior,* June 18, 1947.

28. *El Universal,* January 8, 1947.

29. Comandancia Militar, March 16, 1947, Palo Alto Library.

30. USDA, Ag. Research Ad., May 12, 1949, [Third] California *Senate Report,* p. 39; Schroeder-Lewis Interview.

31. *Excelsior,* June 10, 1947; Interview with Dr. Fred Major, Inspector in Charge of Animal Disease Eradication, USDA, El Paso, Texas, July 16, 1962, hereafter cited as Major Interview; Interview with Dr. Donald M. Williams, Co-Director, CMAPPFA, July 2, 1962, hereafter cited as Williams Interview.

32. Comisión, *La Fiebre Aftosa* (1949), p. 20, *Excelsior,* May 29, June 18, and October 8, 1947; Dirección General de Investigaciones Pecuarias, #211 (n.d.), Camargo Archives; Schroeder-Lewis Interview; Major Interview; Auró Saldaña, *Factores,* p. 26. According to Camargo, news reporters produced such distortions that caused alarm among the peasants, causing government news management to be effectuated by 1948, Camargo Interview; Simms Statement, *House Hearings,* p. 5; USDA, Ag. Research Ad., October 20, 1948, [Second] California *Senate Report,* pp. 41–42; *Novedades,* January 14, 1948.

33. ¿QUE SABE UD. DE LA VACUNA CONTRA LA AFTOSA? (CMAPEFA, n.d.), Palo Alto Library.

34. *El Universal,* April 4, and October 9, 1947; *Novedades,* April 2, 1947; *Excelsior,* October 3, 1947.

35. Camargo Interview.

36. Kirksey, "Reports" of July 11, 1949, and January 10, 1950, [Third] California *Senate Report,* pp. 51, 71; Auró Saldaña, *Factores,* pp. 28–29; *Excelsior,* May 12, July 28, and August 10, 1947.

37. *Ultimas Noticias,* August 28, 1947.

38. *El Universal,* October 9, 1947; *Excelsior,* October 7 and 9, 1947; *La Prensa,* October 9, 1947.

39. *Excelsior,* October 9, 16, 18, 21, 22, 23, 24, and 25, 1947; *La Prensa,* October 9, 1947. The context in which *La Prensa* used *compadrazgo* connotes an indirect form of nepotism even though the *compadre* is not necessarily a blood relative. The implications of *compadrazgo* and extended family relationships are quite numerous and penetrate the very fabric of the Mexican body politic. See Whetten, *Rural Mexico, passim.*

40. H. F. Wilkins, "Report of the Committee on Foot-and-Mouth Disease," United States Livestock Sanitary Association, [Third] California *Senate Report,* pp. 31–2; Schroeder-Lewis Interview.

Chapter V

1. Peru. Ministerio de Agricultura. *Boletín del Instituto Nacional Anti-Aftosa* (January–June, 1949), pp. 23–6.

2. Ecuador. Dirección General de Ganadería y Veterinaria. *La Fiebre Aftosa en el Ecuador: Informe Oficial* (Quito, 1961), pp. i–1, hereafter cited as *La Fiebre Aftosa en Ecuador, 1961.*

3. Ecuador. Centro de Salud Pecuaria (CSP). *Informe de Labores. Mayo 1962–Junio 1963* (Quito, 1963), p. 7, hereafter cited as CSP, *Informe, Mayo 1962–Junio 1963.*

4. *La Fiebre Aftosa en Ecuador, 1961,* pp. 2–4.

5. *Ibid.,* pp. 8, 18–19, 4–7, 21–22, 14–17, 7.

6. *New York Times,* February 27, 1949, November 19, 1950, and April 12, 1951; "Status of Foot-and-Mouth Disease in South and Central America and the Caribbean Area," *JAVMA* (November, 1954), pp. 360–61, hereafter cited as "FMD," *JAVMA.*

7. Colombia. Ministerio de Agricultura. *Fiebre Aftosa en Colombia* (Bogotá, 1952), pp. 10–14.

8. "FMD," *JAVMA,* pp. 360–61.

9. *American Cattle Producer* (April, 1960), p. 27.

10. Carlos Ruíz Martínez. *Veterinaria Venezolana: Treinta años de fomento ganadero, sanidad animal e higiene veterinaria, 1936–1966,* pp. 126–9, hereafter cited as Ruíz Martínez, *Veterinaria Venezolana.* Most of the information for this section came from Ruíz Martínez' definitive work and is amply confirmed by the different

studies of Miguel Villegas, another leading Venezuelan veterinary scientist.

11. *Ibid.,* pp. 363–5, 367.
12. *Ibid.,* pp. 130, 131, 132; Eduardo Mendoza Goiticóa to Junta Revolucionaria, December 16, 1947, and Claudio E. Muskus to Mendoza Goiticóa, December 22, 1947, in *ibid.,* pp. 135–6, 132–4.
13. Rómulo Betancourt to Mendoza Goiticóa, December 24, 1947, in *ibid.,* 137–9.
14. Statement of Dr. Diego Heredia H., President, Veterinary Medical Society, *El Nacional,* December 28, 1947, in *ibid.,* pp. 140–44.
15. *Ibid.,* p. 126.
16. *Ibid.,* pp. 146–59.
17. *Ibid.,* p. 159.
18. *Ibid.,* pp. 150–61; *New York Times,* October 19, 1950.
19. Ruíz Martínez, *Veterinaria Venezolana,* pp. 161–2.
20. *Ibid.,* pp. 163–4.
21. *Ibid.,* pp. 164–5.
22. Venezuela. Instituto de la Fiebre Aftosa. *Boletín Informativo* (May, 1952), pp. 4–5; *Ibid.,* pp. 165–6.
23. Ruíz Martínez, *Veterinaria Venezolana,* p. 166.
24. *Ibid.,* p. 170. Statistical data on annual mortality due to FMD and economic losses can also be found in *ibid.,* pp. 173–7.
25. Traum-Schoening, "Report," p. 8.
26. *Ibid.,* pp. 6, 18.
27. D. Saraiva, "A Febre Aftosa no Rio Grande do Sul, Em 1957," *Boletim do Direcção do Producção Animal* (1959/1960), pp. 42, 44–45.
28. *The New York Times,* December 8, 1948.
29. *Ibid.,* December 18, 1950.
30. Traum-Schoening, "Report," pp. 27–9.
31. SELSA, *Antecedentes.*
32. *The New York Times,* May 18, 1959; Peffer, "FMD in U.S. Policy," p. 141; *American Cattle Producer* (November, 1962), pp. 10–11.
33. Peffer, "FMD in U.S. Policy," pp. 169–70; *American Cattle Producer* (April, 1962), p. 7.
34. Ritchie, "FMD in South America," p. 326.
35. *Ibid.,* pp. 324–6.
36. *Ibid.,* pp. 326–7.
37. *The New York Times,* March 28, 1960.
38. SELSA, *Antecedentes.*
39. *The New York Times,* August 4, 1960.
40. SELSA, *Antecedentes.*
41. *The New York Times,* February 12, 1952.

42. *Ibid.,* August 22, 1951.
43. Pan American Sanitary Bureau. *Director's Report* (Washington, D.C., 1952), p. 19.
44. Pan American Sanitary Bureau. *The Pan American Foot-and Mouth Disease Center. Annual Report, 1952* (Washington, D.C., 1952), pp. 7, 10–11, hereafter cited as PANAFTOSA, Report.
45. *Ibid.* (1951), p. 15.
46. *Ibid.* (1954), pp. 14–15.
47. *Ibid.,* p. 12.
48. *Ibid.* (1955), pp. 23, 10.

Chapter VI

1. *The New York Times,* December 4, 1960.
2. SELSA, *Antecedentes.*
3. *American Cattle Producer* (August, 1961), p. 18.
4. Argentine-United States Joint Commission on Foot-and-Mouth Disease. *Studies on Foot-and-Mouth Disease,* p. v, hereafter cited as Argentine-U.S. Commission, *FMD.*
5. Samuel A. Goldblith, "Foot-and-Mouth Disease: An International Problem," *Food Technologist* (June, 1963), p. 71, hereafter cited as Goldblith, "FMD."
6. *Ibid.; The New York Times,* January 7, 1962; "Editorial: International Diplomacy gives Foot-and-Mouth Disease Research New Impetus," *JAVMA* (October 1, 1962), p. 853.
7. Argentine-U.S. Commission, *FMD,* pp. v-vi.
8. *American Cattle Producer* (January, 1962) and (March, 1962), pp. 6, and 12 respectively.
9. *Ibid.* (April, 1962), pp. 7–8; Argentine-U.S. Commission, FMD, *passim.*
10. *American Cattle Producer* (April, 1962) and (June, 1962), pp. 4 and 10 respectively.
11. *Ibid.,* (September, 1962) and (November, 1962), pp. 16 and 11 respectively; Argentine-U.S. Commission, *FMD,* pp. vi, 49.
12. SELSA, *Antecedentes.*
13. *The New York Times,* February 11, 1963.
14. Goldblith, "FMD," p. 70.
15. Argentine-U.S. Commission, *FMD,* pp. 41, 44.
16. SELSA, *Antecedentes.*
17. Argentine-U.S. Commission, *FMD,* pp. 85–8, 51.
18. *Ibid.,* pp. 69–70.
19. *The New York Times,* July 13, 1963; Goldblith, "FMD," p. 71.
20. *The New York Times,* July 13, and September 1, 1963.
21. SELSA, *Antecedentes.*
22. *Ibid.;* SELSA, *Boletín Epizoötiológico* (Buenos Aires, 1965), p. 2.

23. Seoane and Palacios, *Report,* pp. 17–18.
24. *Ibid.,* pp. 15–16; *IAECOSOC,* p. 2; Pan American Foot-and-Mouth Disease Center, *Cuadernos* (April, 1963), p. 2.
25. Seoane and Palacios, *Report,* p. 16.
26. *Ibid.*
27. *Ibid.*
28. *Ibid.,* p. 17. For a breakdown of each nation's contribution to the support of the FMD Center in Brazil, see Appendix A.
29. Paraguay. Ministerio de Agricultura y Ganadería, "La Fiebre Aftosa: Perentoria necesidad de su control en el Paraguay, Presentado por la Dirección de Ganadería al Segundo Congreso Ganadero del Paraguay," n.d., p. 2. This document was supplied by Dr. Félix Humberto Paiva, Chief, División de Sanidad Animal, Asunción, Paraguay, hereafter cited as "La Fiebre Aftosa: Perentoria Necesidad."
30. *Ibid.,* p. 1.
31. *Ibid.,* p. 2; Félix Humberto Paiva, "La Fiebre Aftosa en el Paraguay: Aspectos Internacionales: Planificación para una Campaña sanitaria a nivel nacional," (March 4, 1966), p. 1, hereafter cited as Paiva, "Le Fiebre Aftosa en el Paraguay," unpublished ms. supplied to the author by Dr. Paiva.
32. "La Fiebre Aftosa: Perentoria Necesidad," pp. 3–4.
33. *Ibid.,* p. 2.
34. *Ibid.,* p. 4.
35. Seoane and Palacios, *Report,* p. 14.
36. *Ibid.,* pp. 14–15.
37. *Ibid.,* p. 15.
38. *Ibid.,* pp. 18–19.
39. *Ibid.,* p. 19.
40. *Ibid.,* pp. 19–20.
41. *Ibid.,* p. 20.
42. *Ibid.,* pp. 20–21.

Chapter VII

1. *IAECOSOC,* p. 1.
2. *Cuadernos* (April, 1963), p. 2.
3. Seoane and Palacios, *Report,* p. 12.
4. *Ibid.,* p. 12.
5. *Ibid.,* pp. 13–14.
6. Ruíz Martínez, *Veterinaria Venezolana,* pp. 166–7.
7. *Ibid.,* pp. 167–8.
8. Venezuela. Instituto de la Fiebre Aftosa. *Boletín Informativo* (January, 1963), pp. 16–18.
9. *Ibid.,* pp. 6–9.
10. Seoane and Palacios, *Report,* p. 11.
11. *Ibid.,* p. 10.

12. *IAECOSOC*, p. 1; *ibid.*, p. 25.

13. Seoane and Palacios, *Report*, p. 25, and Carlos Lleras Restrepo to Seoane and Palacios, February 17, 1967, Anexo 8 in Seoane and Palacios, *Report*.

14. *Ibid.*, pp. 26–7.

15. *Ibid.*, pp. 27–8.

16. *Ibid.*, pp. 25–6, 28–9.

17. CSP, *Informe, Mayo 1961–Junio 1962*, p. 6.

18. *Ibid.*, p. 1; *La Fiebre Aftosa en Ecuador, 1961*, pp. 24–5.

19. CSP, *Informe, Mayo 1961–Junio 1962*, p. 5.

20. *Ibid.*, pp. 1–3.

21. *Ibid.*, pp. 6–7.

22. *Ibid.*, pp. 7–8.

23. Minister of Development, Ecuador, to Minister of Agriculture, Colombia, February 20, 1962, Minister of Agriculture, Colombia, to Minister of Development, Ecuador, March 20, 1962, in *ibid.*, pp. 26, 27.

24. CSP, *Informe, Mayo 1962–Junio 1963*, pp. 9, 12–13.

25. *Ibid.*, pp. 15, 20.

26. *Ibid.*, pp. 9, 11–12.

27. *Ibid.*, pp. 15, 22; Ecuador. Dirección General de Salud Pecuaria. *Programa Nacional de Campaña Antiaftosa* (Quito, 1964), pp. 58–64, hereafter cited as *Programa Nacional*.

28. *Programa Nacional*, p. 67–68.

29. *Ibid.*, p. 19.

30. *Ibid.*, pp. 20–21.

31. *Ibid.*, pp. 29, 38–9, 37, 45.

32. Ecuador. Dirección General de Salud Pecuaria. ECUADOR. *Trabajos Convenio Colombo-Ecuatoriano* (Quito, 1966), p. 2.

33. *Ibid.*, p. 3.

34. *IAECOSOC*, p. 1; Seoane and Palacios, *Report*, pp. 21–2.

35. CSP, *Informe, Mayo 1962–Junio 1963*, p. 21; *Programa Nacional*, pp. 83–6.

36. Seoane and Palacios, *Report*, pp. 21–3.

37. *Ibid.*, pp. 23–4.

38. Argentine-U.S. Commission, FMD, p. 50. For additional details, see *American Cattle Producer* (November, 1962), p. 11, and *Cuadernos* (April, 1963), p. 2.

39. *Cuadernos* (April, 1963), pp. 6–8.

40. Paiva, "Fiebre Aftosa en el Paraguay," p. 2; Pan American Sanitary Bureau, *Annual Report, 1965*, p. 26.

41. Seoane and Palacios, Report, pp. 8, 9.

42. *Ibid.*, pp. 3–4; *The New York Times*, January 4, 1965.

43. Seoane and Palacios, *Report*, pp. 3–4, 37–8.

44. *Ibid.*, pp. 41–3.

45. *Ibid.,* p. 38.
46. *Ibid.,* pp. 39–41.
47. *Ibid.,* p. 39.
48. *Ibid.,* pp. 30–31.
49. *Ibid.,* pp. 26–37.
50. *Ibid.*
51. *Ibid.,* pp. i–ii.

Chapter VIII

1. William H. Henderson, "La Fiebre Aftosa en las Américas," Pan American Sanitary Bureau *Boletín* (November, 1960) pp. 482–4.
2. *Gaceta Veterinaria* (March, April, 1958), p. 7.
3. *Cuadernos,* (May, 1963), p. 1.
4. C. U. Duckworth, "Cooperación Internacional en Vasta Escala: Una realidad demonstrada en el control de la Fiebre Aftosa," Pan American Sanitary Bureau, *Boletín* (September, 1951), pp. 246–7.
5. Seoane and Palacios, *Report,* pp. 52–4.
6. *Ibid.,* pp. 54–5.
7. *Ibid.,* p. 56.
8. *Ibid.,* pp. 57–9.
9. A superb study of the reactions of Latin Americans to the Good Neighbor Policy and its subsequent changes during the 1940s and into the cold war can be found in Donald M. Dozer, *Are We Good Neighbors?* Bryce Wood traces the evolution of the Good Neighbor Policy in his *Making of the Good Neighbor Policy,* showing the factors that eventually became identified with a radical change in attitude by the United States vis-à-vis Latin America.
10. *JAVMA* (October 1, 1962), p. 854.
11. *IAECOSOC,* p. 4.
12. Henderson, "La Fiebre Aftosa," pp. 486–7.
13. Goldblith, "FMD," p. 71.
14. Henderson, "La Fiebre Aftosa," p. 487; Seoane and Palacios, *Report,* pp. 7–8.

BIBLIOGRAPHY

A COMMENT ON SOURCES

Foot-and-mouth disease as a topic for research in inter-American relations has received little attention from historians. The most recent book on the general development of Pan Americanism from its early beginnings to the present is that of Gordon Connell-Smith of the University of Hull, entitled *The Inter-American System,* which fails to mention aftosa even though it does briefly discuss the Pan American Sanitary Bureau. Another general work on United States–Latin American relations, Graham H. Stuart's *Latin America and the United States,* devotes but a single paragraph to the Mexican aftosa problem and completely neglects the conflict between the United States and Argentina.

More recently, J. Lloyd Mecham's *A Survey of United States-Latin American Relations* also devotes only a paragraph to the aftosa outbreak in Mexico. Mecham, however, incorporates the recent scholarship of Bryce Wood's "The Department of State and the Non-National Interest: The Cases of Argentine Meat and Paraguayan Tea," *Inter-American Economic Affairs.* Wood carefully indicates the extent to which advocates of the Good Neighbor Policy were willing to go to carry out their ideas and the powerful forces in the United States that aligned themselves against the United States-Argentine Sanitary Convention. In short, "Good Neighborliness" was suspended when it jeopardized the national interest. In a more general vein, E. Louise Peffer's "Foot-and-Mouth Disease in United States Policy," [Stanford University] *Food Research Institute Studies* shows the economic pressures that were at play in the Smoot-Hawley Tariff Act of 1930 and the agitation over the Sanitary Convention with Argentina. Even though Donald M. Dozer's *Are We Good Neighbors?* fails to mention aftosa in Latin America, his superb analysis of public opinion allows the placing of the FMD problem in a broader context. Bryce Wood's *Making of the Good Neighbor Policy* synthesizes his findings in the previously mentioned article and places the problem in the perspective of the Good Neighbor Policy in general.

Three rather dated works on Argentina, Felix J. Weil, *Argentine Riddle;* John W. White, *Argentina: The Life Story of a Nation;* and Arthur P. Whitaker, *The United States and Argentina,* excoriate the United States' refusal to purchase Argentine meat and its failure to ratify the controversial sanitary convention. All three authors seem to approve the sacrificing of the national interest in an attempt to woo Argentina. In all probability, this is the result, in part, of determination to atone for the past sins of the United States in inter-American relations and, in part, of lack of background in the scientific aspects of aftosa control. On the other hand, Harold F. Peterson's *Argentina and the United States, 1810–1960,* takes a more balanced though general view of the problem. Two Argentines, Alberto Conil Paz and Gustavo Ferrari in their *Argentina's Foreign Policy, 1930–1962,* give an Argentine view of the meat problem. Their account, moreover, is straightforward and uncluttered by vitriolic denunciations of the United States.

Unfortunately, the rest of South America has not received the attention that has been devoted to Argentina's FMD problem and the consequences for inter-American relations. One monumental work, Carlos Ruíz Martínez' *Veterinaria Venezolana: Treinta años de fomento ganadero, sanidad animal e higiene veterinaria, 1936–1966,* is written by a leading Venezuelan veterinarian who has also proven his talents as an historian with this work. He carefully relates the trials of veterinarians in Venezuela to avert aftosa and solidly grounds his work in social and political developments that bear on the introduction and spread of aftosa in his country.

The Mexican-United States cooperative effort has, until recently, received little attention. Fred Gipson's and Bill Leftwich's *The "Cow Killers": With the Aftosa Commission in Mexico* is a highly popularized work that, unfortunately, is marred by gross oversimplification and inaccuracies. Though seemingly unrelated, Oscar Lewis' *Children of Sánchez* offers an incisive view of popular reaction to the aftosa campaign in Mexico. Lewis' work does not contain verifiable historical data, but the *ambiente* of the problem is made manifest. Ramón Auró Saladaña's *Factores que han Influído en la Extensión y la Propagación de la Fiebre Aftosa en Nuestro País* is a doctoral dissertation published as part of the requirement for a veterinary degree at the National Autonomous University of Mexico. Although the work is primarily oriented toward the technical aspects of aftosa, the author is cognizant of the importance of the economic, social, and political factors that militated against the rapid control and eradication of the disease in Mexico. Unfortunately, Howard F. Cline's *United States and Mexico,* an otherwise excellent work, is marred by inaccuracies regarding aftosa. Some of these inaccuracies may be the result of some sources being unavailable. Yet, Dr. Cline seems to allow his own biases to condemn prematurely the *Sinarquistas* for their opposition to United

States participation in the campaign. Two works by Manuel A. Machado, Jr., *"Aftosa* and the Mexican-United States Sanitary Convention of 1928," in *Agricultural History* and *An Industry in Crisis: Mexican-United States Cooperation in the Control of Foot-and-Mouth Disease* analyze the role of FMD in United States-Mexican relations. The second work demonstrates how national self-interest worked to draw both countries closer together.

In general, foot-and-mouth disease provides a valuable focus for the study of inter-American relations, even though the technical aspects of the problem may discourage scholars. Nonetheless, the historical profession would do well to follow the dictum of Hans Zinsser in his *Rats, Lice, and History* which first appeared in 1934. Zinsser noted the importance of disease in the history of civilization and emphasized the importance of its study for general and specialized works. Scholars should, therefore, expand beyond the more traditional approaches to history and relate disease to the social, economic, and political problems that afflict the history of Latin America.

1. UNPUBLISHED MANUSCRIPT MATERIALS:

Anderson, R. J., to Manuel A. Machado, Jr., July 11, 1961.

Argentina. Secretaría de Estado de Agricultura y Ganadería de la Nación, Dirección General de Sanidad Animal, Servicio de Luchas Sanitarias (SELSA). *Antecedentes Cronológicos de la Lucha Contra la Fiebre Aftosa* (limited circulation manuscript)

Camargo Núñez, Fernando, Archives. This archival material was made available to the author by the late Dr. Camargo during the author's two visits to Mexico City in 1962 and 1963. For specific references to the material contained in the collection, see footnotes.

Mexico. Dirección General de Investigaciones Pecuarias, Library, Palo Alto, D.F. This fine collection of materials was obtained through the auspices of Dr. Fernando Díaz Muñoz. Chief of the Vaccine Production Division of the Dirección General.

Paiva, Felix Humberto, "La Fiebre Aftosa en el Paraguay: Aspectos Internacionales: Planificación para una campaña sanitaria a nivel nacional," March 14, 1966. This excellent outline of Paraguayan plans for control and ultimate eradication of FMD was supplied by Dr. Paiva.

Paraguay. Ministerio de Agricultura y Ganadería, "La Fiebre Aftosa: Perentoria necesidad de su control en el Paraguay," Presentado por la Dirección de Ganadería al Segundo Congreso Ganadero del Paraguay. Dr. Paiva also supplied this material, 1966.

United States. Records of the Department of State, Record Group 59. These contain an invaluable collection of documents for the study of aftosa in Latin America. See footnotes for specific references.

Traum, Jacob, and H. W. Schoening, "Report on a Visit to Foot-and-

Mouth Disease Institutes in South America," 1951. An unpublished manuscript supplied by Dr. Raymond A. Bankowski of the School of Veterinary Medicine, University of California, Davis.

2. INTERVIEWS:

Camargo Núñez, Fernando. Typescript of conversation in possession of the author, June 25, 1962.

De la Torre Zarza, Luis. Typescript of conversation in possession of the author, June 25, 1963.

Major, Fred J., Inspector in charge of Animal Disease Eradication, USDA, El Paso, Texas. Typescript of conversation in possession of the author, July 16, 1962.

Schroeder, Robert J. and Cecil Lewis, Taperecording of conversation in possession of the author, September 11, 1961.

Williams, Donald M., Typescript of conversation in possession of the author, July 2, 1962.

3. GOVERNMENT PUBLICATIONS:

Argentina

Dirección de Sanidad Animal. *Lucha Contra la Fiebre Aftosa.* Buenos Aires: n.p., 1945.

Secretaría de Estado de Agricultura y Ganadería de la Nación. Dirección General de Sanidad Animal. Servicio de Luchas Sanitarias (SELSA). *Boletín Epizoötiológico.* Buenos Aires: Secretaría de Agricultura y Ganadería, 1965.

Secretaría de Agricultura y Ganadería. *Instituto de Fiebre Aftosa.* Buenos Aires: n.p., n.d.

Chile

Consejo Superior de Hijiene. *La Fiebre Aftosa del Ganado.* Santiago: n.p., 1910.

Colombia

Ministerio de Agricultura. *Fiebre Aftosa en Colombia.* Bogotá: n.p., 1952.

Ecuador

Centro de Salud Pecuaria. *Informe a la Nación, Mayo 1961–Junio 1962.* Quito: Ministerio de Fomento, August 1962.

―――. *Informe de Labores, Mayo 1962–Junio 1963.* Quito: Centro de Salud Pecuaria, 1963. This particular publication contains an excellent appendix giving detailed information on vaccination and campaign costs.

Dirección General de Ganadería y Veterinaria. *La Fiebre Aftosa en el Ecuador. Informe Oficial.* Quito: Ministerio de Fomento, 1961. Mimeograph.

Dirección General de Salud Pecuaria. *ECUADOR: Trabajos Convenio Colombo-Ecuatoriano.* Quito: Dirección General de Salud Pecuaria, 1966.

Dirección General de Salud Pecuaria. *Programa Nacional de Campaña Antiaftosa.* Quito: Ministerio de Fomento, 1964.

Mexico

Comisión contra la Fiebre Aftosa. *Programa para la Erradicación de la Fiebre Aftosa.* México, D.F.: n.p., 1948.

―――. *Investigación Científica de la Fiebre Aftosa en México.* México, D.F.: n.p., 1948.

―――. *La Campaña Contra la Fiebre Aftosa.* México, D.F.: n.p., 1949.

―――. *La Fiebre Aftosa en México, (Estado Actual de la Campaña).* México, D.F.: n.p., 1951.

Paraguay

Paiva, Félix Humberto. *La Fiebre Aftosa en Números: Severo Impacto en la Economía Pecuaria Latino-Americana.* Asunción: Ministerio de Agricultura y Ganadería, 1964. Mimeograph.

Peru

Ministerio de Agricultura. *Boletín del Instituto Nacional Anti-Aftosa.* See footnotes for citations.

United States

California. Partial Report of the Senate Interim Committee on Livestock Diseases by Senators George P. Hatfield and Harold J. Powers. *Report on Foot and Mouth Disease.* Sacramento: Senate of the State of California, 1948, 1949, and 1951. These three reports contain extremely valuable appendices containing documentary material on outbreaks in California and especially on the Mexican outbreak.

United States Congress. "The Campaign Against Foot-and-Mouth Disease," *Report of the Subcommittee on Foot-and-Mouth Disease of the Committee of Agriculture,* House of Representatives, 80th Congress, First Session, July 17, 1947. Washington, D.C.: Government Printing Office, 1947.

United States Congress. *Congressional Record.* See footnotes for specific citations.

U. S. Congress. "Eradication of Foot-and-Mouth Disease," *Hearings Before a Subcommittee of the Committee of Agriculture,* House of Representatives, 80th Congress, First Session, December 3, 4, and 5, 1947. Washington, D.C.: Government Printing Office, 1948.

U. S. Congress. *Report #1425,* House of Representatives. 80th Congress, Second Session, February 26, 1948. Washington, D.C.: Government Printing Office, 1948.

United States Congress. "Control of Foot-and-Mouth Disease," *Report of a Special Subcommittee to the Committee on Appropriations,* Senate, Document #211, 80th Congress, Second Session. Washington, D.C.: Government Printing Office, 1948.

United States Department of Agriculture. *Foot-and-Mouth Disease.*

Farmer's Bulletin #666. Washington, D.C.: Government Printing Office, 1952.

United States Department of State. *Foreign Relations of the United States.* See footnotes for specific citations.

United States Department of State. *Treaties and other International Acts, Series 2404. Eradication of Foot-and-Mouth Disease in Mexico.* Washington, D.C.: Government Printing Office, 1953.

Venezuela

Instituto de la Fiebre Aftosa. *Boletín Informativo.* Caracas: Instituto de la Fiebre Aftosa, January 1963.

Bilateral and Multilateral Organizations

Argentine-United States Joint Commission on Foot-and-Mouth Disease. *Studies on Foot-and-Mouth Disease.* Washington, D.C.: National Academy of Sciences-National Research Council, 1966.

Inter American Economic and Social Council. "The Economic Importance of Foot-and-Mouth Disease in the Americas," *Second Annual Meeting of the Inter American Economic and Social Council at the Expert and at the Ministerial Level. October–November, 1963, São Paulo, Brazil.* Washington, D.C.: Pan American Union, 1963.

Pan American Sanitary Bureau. *The Pan American Foot-and-Mouth Disease Center. Annual Reports for 1952, 1954, 1955, 1957, 1958, 1959, 1960.* Miscellaneous Publication #11. Washington, D.C. Pan American Sanitary Bureau, 1953, 1955, 1956, 1958, 1959, 1960, 1961.

Pan American Sanitary Bureau. *Director's Report.* Washington, D.C.: Pan American Sanitary Bureau, 1951.

Pan American Sanitary Bureau. *Annual Report of the Director, 1965.* Washington, D.C.: Pan American Sanitary Bureau, August 1966.

Report of the Delegates of the United States of America to the Sixth International Conference of American States, Habana, Cuba, January 16, to February 20, 1928. Washington, D.C.: Government Printing Office, 1928.

Seoane, Edgardo, and Carlos Palacios, Pan American Health Organization. *Report on Foot-and-Mouth Disease, Present and Future Problems on the American Continent, and the Importance of the Pan American Foot-and-Mouth Disease Center.* Washington, D.C.: Pan American Union, 1967.

4. CONTEMPORARY PUBLISHED ACCOUNTS:

Granato, Lourenço. *A Febre Aphtosa.* São Paulo: Pocai-Weiss, 1913.

Griffin, C. *Fiebre Aftosa*. La Plata: Talleres de Publicación del Muséo, 1900.

Mollin, F. E. *The Outbreak of Foot-and-Mouth Disease in Mexico*. Denver: American National Livestock Association, 1947.

Porter, James A. *Doctor, Spare My Cow*. Ames, Iowa: Iowa State College Press, 1956.

Quesada Bravo, Guillermo. *La Verdad Sobre el Ganado Cebú Brasileño, la Fiebre Aftosa y la Cuarentena en la Isla de Sacrificios*. México, D.F.: n.p., 1946.

5. JOURNALS AND ARTICLES:

Agriculture in the Americas. Unless otherwise noted in this bibliography, see notes for specific citations of this journal.

American Brahman Journal, October, 1948.

American Cattle Producer: The Cattleman's Business Magazine. Unless otherwise noted in this bibliography, see notes for specific citations of this journal.

Brock, Elmer, "Some Observations on a South American Trip," *American Cattle Producer*. August, 1941.

Cuadernos, published by the Pan American Foot-and-Mouth Disease Center. See notes for specific reference to this journal.

Duckworth, C. U., "Cooperación Internacional en Vasta Escala: Una Realidad Demonstrada en el Control de la Fiebre Aftosa," Pan American Sanitary Bureau. *Boletín*. September, 1951.

Goldblith, Samuel A., "Foot-and-Mouth Disease: An International Problem," *Food Technology,* June, 1963.

Henderson, William M., "La Fiebre Aftosa en las Américas," Pan American Sanitary Bureau. *Boletín*. November, 1960.

Hopkins, John A., "Fight Against Hoof-and-Mouth Disease in Mexico," *Agriculture in the Americas,* June–July, 1947.

Journal of the American Veterinary Medical Association. For specific references, see notes.

"La Fiebre Aftosa y Nuestro Comercio de Carnes con el Reino Unido," *Revista de Medicina Veterinaria* (Buenos Aires). July, 1936.

Machado, Manuel A., Jr., *"Aftosa* and the Mexican-United States Sanitary Convention of 1928," *Agricultural History,* October, 1965.

Miller, A. W., "Foot-and-Mouth Disease in the United States," *Year Book of Agriculture, 1926* (Washington, D.C.: Government Printing Office, 1927).

Pan American Sanitary Bureau. *Boletín*. Unless otherwise specified in this bibliography, see notes for specific references.

Peffer, E. Louise, "Foot-and-Mouth Disease in United States Policy," [Stanford University] *Food Research Institute Studies,* May, 1962.

Poole, James E., "Persistent Argentina Seeks Our Markets," *American Cattle Producer*. April, 1939.
Ritchie, J. N., "Foot-and-Mouth Disease in South America," [England] *The Journal of the Ministry of Agriculture and Fisheries*. November, 1959.
Saraiva, D., "A Febre Aftosa no Rio Grande do Sul, Em 1957," *Boletim da Direcção do Producção Animal* (Porto Alegre, Rio Grande do Sul, Brazil). 1959/1960.
Shahan, Maurice, "Foot-and-Mouth Disease: One of the Most Important of Infections of Animals," *American Cattle Producer*, March, 1952.
Smith, Mervin G., "The Mexican Beef Cattle Industry," *Foreign Agriculture*, November, 1944.
Wood, Bryce, "The Department of State and the Non-National Interest: The Cases of Argentine Meat and Paraguayan Tea," *Inter-American Economic Affairs*, Autumn, 1961.

6. BOOKS:

Auró Saldaña, Ramón, *Factores que han Influído en la Extensión y la Propagación de la Fiebre Aftosa en Nuestro País*. México, D.F.: Escuela Nacional de Medicina Veterinaria y Zoötécnia, Universidad Nacional Autónoma Mexicana, 1947.
Cline, Howard F. *The United States and Mexico*. New York, Atheneum Books, 1963.
Conil Paz, Alberto, and Gustavo Ferrari. *Argentina's Foreign Policy, 1930–1962*. South Bend, Indiana, University of Notre Dame Press, 1966, translated by John J. Kennedy.
Connell-Smith, Gordon. *The Inter-American System*, Royal Institute of International Affairs, New York, Oxford University Press, 1966.
Dozer, Donald M. *Are We Good Neighbors?: Three Decades of Inter-American Relations, 1930–1960*. Gainesville, University of Florida Press, 1959.
Gipson, Fred, and Bill Leftwich. *The "Cow Killers": With the Aftosa Commission in Mexico*. Austin, University of Texas Press, 1956.
Lewis, Oscar. *Children of Sánchez: The Autobiography of a Mexican Family*. New York, Random House, 1961.
Machado, Manuel A., Jr., *An Industry in Crisis: Mexican-United States Cooperation in the Control of Foot-and-Mouth Disease*, University of California Publications in History, Vol. 80. Berkeley, University of California Press, 1968.
Mecham, J. Lloyd. *A Survey of United States-Latin American Relations*. New York, Houghton-Mifflin, 1965.
Peterson, Harold F., *Argentina and the United States, 1810–1960*. Albany, State University of New York Press, 1964.
Richelet, Juan E. *The Argentine Meat Trade: Meat Inspection Regulations in the Argentine Republic*. London, n.p., 1929.

Ruíz Martínez, Carlos. *Veterinaria Venezolana: Treinta Años de fomento ganadero, sanidad animal e higiene veterinaria, 1936–1966.* Caracas, Editorial Sucre, 1966.

Seltzer, R. E., and T. M. Stubblefield. *Marketing Mexican Cattle in the United States.* Technical Bulletin #142. Tucson, University of Arizona Press, 1960.

Stuart, Graham H. *Latin America and the United States.* New York, Appleton-Century-Crofts, 1955.

Weil, Felix J. *Argentine Riddle.* New York, John Day Co., 1944.

Whetten, Nathan L. *Rural Mexico.* Chicago, University of Chicago Press, 1948.

Whitaker, Arthur P. *The United States and Argentina.* Cambridge, Harvard University Press, 1954.

White, John W. *Argentina: The Life Story of a Nation.* New York, The Viking Press, 1942.

Wood, Bryce. *The Making of the Good Neighbor Policy.* New York, Columbia University Press, 1961.

Zinsser, Hans. *Rats, Lice, and History.* New York, Bantam Books, 1960.

7. NEWSPAPERS:

See notes for specific references to the newspapers listed below.

El Universal (Mexico City)
Excelsior (Mexico City)
La Prensa (Mexico City)
The New York Times
Novedades (Mexico City)
Ultimas Noticias (Mexico City)

Articles from *La Prensa* (Buenos Aires), *El Diario* (Buenos Aires), *La Mañana* (Montevideo), and others cited in the notes were found in the Records of the Department of State and are not, therefore, listed in the bibliography. See notes for these references.

INDEX

A Febre Aphtosa, publication of, 17

Africa, 119

Aftosa Institute, creation of, 5, 40, 66

Agency for International Development (AID), 81, 95, 105

agrarian economy, ruin of, 33, 47, 63

Agricultural Bank (*Banco Agrícola y Pecuaria*), Venezuela, 64-65

Agricultural and Livestock Society of Osorio Province, 35

Agricultural Research, General Directorate of, 43-44, 47, 118

agricultural wealth, 26, 65, 77, 88

Agriculture, Department of, New York State, 118

Agriculture, Department of, United States, 6, 11-13, 16-21, 25, 30-34, 39-42, 46, 70, 78-82, 105; officials of, 5, 9, 11, 15, 31, 45, 82, 105, 111-12

Agriculture, Ministry of, Latin American countries, 21-22, 35, 44, 62, 64-67, 89; officials of, 8, 16, 86, 90, 93, 95, 101, 105

Agriculture and Fisheries, Ministry of, Great Britain, 6

Aguascalientes, state of, 44

air traffic, Mexican, 49

Alagôas, Brazil, 34

Alba, Dr. Aurelio Málaga, Peruvian veterinarian, 61

Alemán Valdés, Miguel, President of Mexico, supports CMAPEFA, 39, 44, 53, 56

Alemán-Ortiz Garza Plan, 40

Alliance for Progress, purpose of, 77-78; problems of, 90, 103, 112, 115, 119

Alpargatón, Venezuela, 67

American Cattle Producer, cited, 25, 27-28, 80-81

American National Cattlemen's Association, 8o

American National Livestock Association, 25, 31

American Republics, Division of, U.S. Department of State, 27

American Veterinary Medical Association, 113-14; Journal of, 79

Amsterdam, Holland, 66

Andean Cordillera Mountains, 34-35, 100, 108

Animal Health Institute, Colombia, 94

Animal Health Organization, Bolivia, 103